Syruplicious: Homemade Recipes for Sweetening Your Life

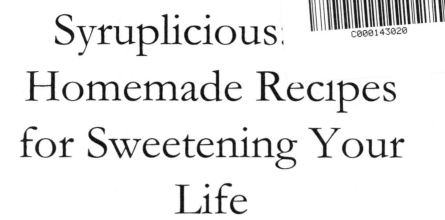
The Wholesome Whisk Nobi

Contents

INTRODUCTION 7

1. Classic Maple Syrup...9

2. Blueberry Syrup..9

3. Strawberry Syrup...10

4. Raspberry Syrup..11

5. Chocolate Syrup..12

6. Caramel Syrup 12

7. Vanilla Syrup 13

8. Peach Syrup 14

9. Blackberry Syrup...15

10. Coconut Syrup 15

11. Cherry Syrup 16

12. Apple Cinnamon Syrup 17

13. Lemon Syrup...18

14. Pineapple Syrup 18

15. Orange Syrup 19

16. Almond Syrup...20

17. Hazelnut Syrup 20

18. Lavender Syrup 21

19. Mint Syrup..22

20. Ginger Syrup 23

21. Honey Syrup..23

22. Espresso Syrup 24

23. Pomegranate Syrup 25

24. Watermelon Syrup...26

25. Rose Syrup...26

26. Banana Syrup 27

27. Mango Syrup 28

28. Passion Fruit Syrup 29

29. Pistachio Syrup 29

30. Cardamom Syrup 30

31. Elderflower Syrup 31

32. Cherry Blossom Syrup 31

33. Hibiscus Syrup 32

34. Pumpkin Spice Syrup 33

35. Cranberry Syrup 34

36. Guava Syrup 35

37. Kiwi Syrup 35

38. Tangerine Syrup 36

39. Butterscotch Syrup 37

40. Grape Syrup 38

41. Fig Syrup 39

42. Cinnamon Syrup 40

43. Irish Cream Syrup 40

44. Salted Caramel Syrup 41

45. Pear Syrup 42

46. Apricot Syrup 43

47. Rosemary Syrup 44

48. Coconut Lime Syrup 44

49. White Chocolate Syrup 45

50. Gingerbread Syrup 46

51. Blueberry Lemon Syrup 47

52. Mint Chocolate Syrup 47

53. Blackcurrant Syrup 48

54. Praline Syrup 49

55. Blood Orange Syrup 50

56. Toasted Marshmallow Syrup 51

57. Cherry Vanilla Syrup 51

58. Lychee Syrup 52

59. Raspberry Lime Syrup 53

60. Earl Grey Syrup 54

61. Pumpkin Caramel Syrup..54

62. Saffron Syrup 55

63. Kiwi Strawberry Syrup...56

64. Apple Pie Syrup 57

65. Salted Caramel Mocha Syrup..57

66. Maple Pecan Syrup...58

67. Brown Sugar Syrup 59

68. Passionfruit Mango Syrup 60

69. Rosewater Syrup 61

70. Ginger Lemongrass Syrup..61

71. Pineapple Coconut Syrup..62

72. Pistachio Rose Syrup...63

73. Honey Lavender Syrup 64

74. Raspberry White Chocolate Syrup.....................................65

75. Blood Orange Elderflower Syrup 65

76. Maple Bacon Syrup 66

77. Amaretto Syrup...67

78. Chai Spice Syrup 68

79. Cherry Limeade Syrup 69

80. Fig Vanilla Syrup 70

81. Blackberry Mint Syrup...70

82. Lemon Blueberry Syrup 71

83. Ginger Plum Syrup..72

84. Caramel Macchiato Syrup 73

85. Raspberry Hibiscus Syrup 74

86. Lavender Vanilla Syrup..74

87. Coconut Pineapple Syrup..75

88. Pistachio Cardamom Syrup 76

89. Mango Passionfruit Syrup...77

90. Praline Pecan Syrup..78

91. Blackberry Sage Syrup 78

92. Maple Walnut Syrup..79

93. Brown Butter Syrup 80

94. Peach Ginger Syrup 80

95. Cherry Almond Syrup..81

96. Lemon Ginger Syrup 82

97. Raspberry Rose Syrup..83

98. Pineapple Mango Syrup...84

99. Pistachio Almond Syrup..84

100. Apple Caramel Syrup..85

101. Maple Bourbon Syrup 86

CONCLUSION...88

INTRODUCTION

Syruplicious: 101 Homemade Recipes for Sweetening Your Life is the perfect cookbook for anyone looking to make delicious treats with the simple sweetness of syrup. From pancakes and waffles to pastries and hot drinks, this book provides easy-to-follow recipes and simple tips for turning everyday ingredients into something extraordinary. With helpful photographs and detailed instructions, anyone can make a mouth-watering syrup-flavored dish that's sure to please.

The book begins with an exploration of the many types of syrups available, as well as their history and cultural context. From regional specialties to exotic creations, there is something for everyone. Many recipes include detailed step-by-step instructions, so even the novice cook can master the art of syrup-making.

To make everything even sweeter, the book also includes delicious recipes for all sorts of syrups, from traditional fruit to herb-infused and chocolate-based combinations. You can create sauces for ice cream sundaes, waffles, and pancakes, or layer it onto cakes or pies. You can bake muffins, cakes, and cookies with unique flavor combinations, making it easy to impress guests or clients.

Next, the book introduces readers to a wide variety of drinks that can be sweetened with syrup. From smoothies and shakes to lattes and cocktails, these recipes will help you make drinks that are truly unique. You'll learn how to make tasty and visually appealing combinations of syrups, fruits, spices, and herbs.

Finally, there are recipes for homemade gifts such as syrups and preserves. Imagine gifting friends with a jar of homemade maple syrup or a bottle of berry-infused syrup. It will make great gifts for birthdays, anniversaries, and other special occasions. Plus, you can even get creative and upscale favorite recipes with fancy syrups.

Overall, Syruplicious provides all the tools and recipes you need to make amazing and delicious dishes and drinks with syrup. No matter what your taste, you'll enjoy sweetening your life with this book!

1. Classic Maple Syrup

Classic Maple Syrup is a simple yet delicious breakfast topping, featuring the flavors of pure maple syrup. This easy recipe provides all the sweetness you need for a start to a great day.
Serving: 4
Preparation Time: 5 minutes
Ready Time: 5 minutes

Ingredients:
- 1 cup pure maple syrup
- 2 tablespoons butter
- Pinch of salt

Instructions:
1. In a saucepan, bring the maple syrup to a low simmer.
2. Add in the butter and a pinch of salt and stir until melted.
3. Simmer for 4-5 minutes until it thickens.
4. Transfer to a small bowl to cool slightly before serving.

Nutrition information: per serving (1/4 cup): Calories 200; Total Fat 0.6g (saturated fat 0.4g); Cholesterol 6mg; Sodium 105mg; Total carbohydrates 50.7g (dietary fibre 0.1g); Protein 0.3g

2. Blueberry Syrup

This easy to prepare Blueberry Syrup is a delicious addition to any breakfast or dessert.
Serving: 4-6
Preparation Time: 5 minutes
Ready Time: 25 minutes

Ingredients:
 2 cups fresh blueberries
 1/4 cup granulated sugar
 2 tablespoons lemon juice

Instructions:

1. In a small saucepan over medium-high heat, add the blueberries. Cover with a lid and let cook for 3-5 minutes, stirring occasionally, until the blueberries break down and release their juice.
2. Add the sugar and lemon juice to the saucepan and stir well. Decrease the heat to low and simmer the blueberry mixture for 15 minutes.
3. Strain the syrup using a fine mesh sieve, pushing down on the blueberries to remove as much liquid as possible.
4. Let the syrup cool before serving.

Nutrition information: Serving size 1/4 cup, 67 calories, 0g fat, 17.4g carbohydrates, 0.3g protein, 0mg cholesterol, 0.7mg sodium, 1.2g dietary fiber.

3. Strawberry Syrup

This delicious strawberry syrup recipe will become a favorite with the whole family. Perfect for topping on pancakes or waffles, adding to lemonade or yogurt, or for making simply delightful strawberry sundaes.
Serving: 8
Preparation Time: 10 minutes
Ready Time: 45 minutes

Ingredients:
- 2 cups of ripe strawberries
- 3/4 cup of granulated sugar
- 2 tablespoons of lemon juice
- 1/4 teaspoon of kosher salt

Instructions:
1. In a small bowl, mash the strawberries until they are slightly chunky.
2. In a medium saucepan, combine mashed strawberries, sugar, lemon juice, and salt.
3. Bring to a low simmer over low heat, stirring often until mixture thickens. This should take about 40 minutes.
4. Strain syrup with a fine mesh strainer into a bowl and discard the solids.
5. Let syrup cool, then pour into a jar for storing.

Nutrition information:
Calories: 41 kcal, Carbohydrates: 10.5 g, Protein: 0.2 g, Fat: 0.1 g,
Saturated Fat: 0.1 g, Sodium: 510 mg, Potassium: 23 mg, Fiber: 0.3 g,
Sugar: 8.7 g, Vitamin A: 5 IU, Vitamin C: 9.2 mg, Calcium: 6 mg, Iron:
0.1 mg

4. Raspberry Syrup

Raspberry Syrup is a sweet sauce prepared with raspberry juice and sugar.
It has a deep sweet flavor and a vibrant red color which makes it ideal for
topping pancakes, waffles and ice creams.
Serving: 4-6
Preparation time: 10 minutes
Ready time: 10 minutes

Ingredients:
- 2 cups of fresh raspberry juice
- 2-3 cups of sugar
- 1 teaspoon of lemon juice

Instructions:
1. In a medium saucepan, bring the raspberry juice and sugar to a boil.
2. Reduce the heat to low and simmer for 5 minutes stirring occasionally.
3. Add the lemon juice and stir and simmer for 2 more minutes.
4. Remove from heat and strain the syrup into a container.
5. Allow the raspberry syrup to cool before using.

Nutrition information:
Serving Size: 1 tablespoon (15 ml)
Calories: 21
Total Fat: 0 g
Sodium: 0 mg
Total Carbohydrates: 5 g
Protein: 0 g

5. Chocolate Syrup

Chocolate Syrup is the perfect treat for those hot summer days or to use in baking delicious dessert concoctions. It is an easy way to take your favourite desserts to the next level!
Serving: 4-6 servings
Preparation time: 5 minutes
Ready time: 10 minutes

Ingredients:
• 1/4 cup unsweetened cocoa powder
• 1/2 cup granulated sugar
• 1/2 cup light corn syrup
• 1/4 cup water
• 1 teaspoon pure vanilla extract

Instructions:
1. In a small saucepan, whisk together the cocoa powder, sugar, corn syrup and water.
2. Place the pan over medium-high heat and bring to a boil.
3. Reduce the heat to medium low and simmer for 5 minutes, stirring occasionally.
4. Remove the pan from the heat and stir in the vanilla extract until combined.
5. Let the mixture cool for 5 minutes, then pour into an airtight container and store in the refrigerator until ready to use.

Nutrition information:
Calories: 79 kcal, Carbohydrates: 19 g, Protein: 0.3 g, Fat: 0.1 g, Saturated Fat: 0.1 g, Sodium: 2 mg, Potassium: 20 mg, Fiber: 0.1 g, Sugar: 16 g, Vitamin A: 1.6 IU, Calcium: 3.2 mg, Iron: 0.2 mg

6. Caramel Syrup

Caramel syrup is a delicious and sweet topping for all kinds of desserts, pancakes and ice creams. It is a fusion of sugar and butter that turns into a thick and sticky syrup.
Serving: 4

Preparation Time: 10 minutes
Ready Time: 10 minutes

Ingredients:
- 1/2 cup of salted butter
- 1/2 cup of packed brown sugar
- 1/4 cup of light corn syrup
- 2 tablespoons of heavy cream

Instructions:
1. Place the butter into a medium-sized pot and melt it over low heat.
2. Add the brown sugar, light corn syrup, and heavy cream.
3. Whisk constantly until all the Ingredients are combined and the mixture begins to bubble.
4. Simmer for 5 minutes while stirring constantly, then remove from heat.
5. Let cool for 3 minutes before pouring into an airtight container for storage.

Nutrition information: Calories: 176 per serving
Total Fat: 11.3 g per serving
Total Carbohydrates: 21.9 g per serving
Protein: 0.3 g per serving

7. Vanilla Syrup

Vanilla Syrup is a creamy, sweet syrup made with pure vanilla extract and sugar. It is perfect for adding flavor to beverages, desserts and your favorite cooking and baking recipes.
Serving: 8 servings
Preparation Time: 10 minutes
Ready Time: 10 minutes

Ingredients:
- 1 cup granulated sugar
- 1 cup water
- 4 teaspoons pure vanilla extract

Instructions:
1. Place the sugar and water in a medium saucepan over medium-high heat. Stir until the sugar dissolves.
2. Bring the mixture to a simmer and cook for 3-4 minutes, stirring occasionally, until the syrup is slightly thickened.
3. Add the vanilla extract and stir to combine.
4. Remove from the heat and cool completely before transferring the syrup to a jar or air-tight container.

Nutrition information
Per serving: Calories: 70; Fat: 0.3g; Carbs: 17.1g; Protein: 0.2g

8. Peach Syrup

This homemade Peach Syrup is sweet and lightly spiced with cinnamon. The perfect topping for your pancakes, oatmeal and waffles or even for your breakfast yogurt.
Serving: 18 tablespoons
Preparation time: 10 minutes
Ready time: 25 minutes

Ingredients:
- 2 peaches, cut into thin slices
- 1 cup granulated sugar
- 2/3 cup water
- 1 teaspoon ground cinnamon

Instructions:
1. In a medium saucepan, add the peach slices, sugar, water and cinnamon.
2. Mix gently over a low-medium heat and let cook for about 10 minutes, stirring continuously.
3. Once the peach Syrup reaches a syrup-like consistency, remove from heat and let cool for 15 minutes before serving.

Nutrition information: per tablespoon (18 servings): 60 calories, 0g fat, 15g carbohydrates, 0g protein, 0mg sodium, 0g fiber.

9. Blackberry Syrup

Delicious Blackberry Syrup is the perfect way to add both sweetness and flavor to your favorite pancakes and waffles for breakfast.
Serving: Makes about 3 cups (750mls) syrup
Preparation time: 10 minutes
Ready time: 25 minutes

Ingredients:
• 2 (12 ounce/ 375g) boxes of blackberries
• 2 1/2 cups (625mls) of water
• 2 cups (400g) granulated sugar
• 2 tablespoons (30 ml) freshly squeezed lemon juice

Instructions:
1. In a medium saucepan, combine the blackberries, water and sugar.
2. Place over high heat and bring to a boil, stirring occasionally.
3. Reduce heat to medium and simmer uncovered for 15 minutes, stirring occasionally.
4. Remove from heat and mash the berries with a potato masher, whisk or fork.
5. Strain through a fine mesh strainer and stir in lemon juice.
6. Cool to room temperature and transfer to a jar or other airtight container.

Nutrition information: Per serving, Blackberry Syrup contains approximately 130 calories, 0g total fat, 0g saturated fat, 0mg cholesterol, 10mg sodium, 33g carbohydrates, 1g protein, and 1g dietary fiber.

10. Coconut Syrup

Coconut Syrup is a delicious recipe with coconut flavor. Its thick and sweet texture works best as a topping for pancakes and waffles, as well as in many mixed beverages.
Serving: Around 8-10 servings
Preparation Time: 10 minutes

Ready Time: 30 minutes

Ingredients:
* 1 cup white sugar
* 1 cup water
* 1 cup shredded or flaked coconut

Instructions:
1. In a small saucepan, combine sugar and water.
2. Heat the mixture over medium heat, stirring occasionally, until the sugar has dissolved.
3. Increase the heat to high and bring mixture to a boil. Boil for 3 minutes, stirring constantly.
4. Reduce the heat to low and add the shredded coconut. Simmer for 3-5 minutes, stirring constantly, until the syrup has thickened.
5. Remove from heat and let cool.
6. Pour the cooled syrup into a container and store in an airtight container in the fridge.

Nutrition information:
Serving size: 2 tablespoons; Calories: 85; Fat: 0.1g; Carbs: 21.8g; Sugars: 21.4g; Fiber: 0.4g; Protein: 0.1g; Sodium: 0.1mg

11. Cherry Syrup

This recipe creates a simple and sweet cherry syrup that is perfect for topping your favorite desserts, drinks, or even morning pancakes!
Serving: Makes 1-2 servings
Preparation Time: 5 minutes
Ready Time: 10 minutes

Ingredients:
- 1 cup fresh or frozen cherries
- ¼ cup sugar
- 2 tablespoons water

Instructions:
1. Place the cherries, sugar, and water in a small pot.

2. Simmer over medium heat until the cherries are soft and the sugar has dissolved, about 5 minutes.
3. Once everything has dissolved, use a spoon or fork to mash the cherries.
4. Continue simmering for 5 minutes more to reduce the mixture.
5. Strain the syrup through a fine-mesh sieve.
6. Let cool and transfer to an airtight container.

Nutrition information: Calories: 128, Total Fat: 0.2g, Sodium: 1.3mg, Total Carbohydrate: 35.7g, Protein: 0.6g.

12. Apple Cinnamon Syrup

Apple Cinnamon Syrup is an amazing recipe, with enhanced flavour of cinnamon. It has sweetness of apples and a pinch of warm cinnamon taste.
Serving: 4
Preparation time: 10 minutes
Ready time: 25 minutes

Ingredients:
- 2 cups water
- 2 cups organic sugar
- 2 medium size apples – peeled, cored, chopped
- 2 teaspoons ground cinnamon

Instructions:
1. In a medium-sized saucepan, bring water to a boil.
2. Add sugar, apples, and cinnamon, reduce heat and cook over medium heat for about 10 minutes, stirring occasionally.
3. Remove from heat and strain into a large bowl.
4. Let cool and enjoy with your favourite breakfast treats.

Nutrition information:
Calories: 217 kcal, Carbohydrates: 55 g, Protein: 0 g, Fat: 0 g, Saturated Fat: 0 g, Sodium: 5 mg, Potassium: 52 mg, Fiber: 2 g, Sugar: 51 g, Vitamin A: 5 IU, Vitamin C: 3.5 mg, Calcium: 6 mg, Iron: 0.3 mg

13. Lemon Syrup

Lemon Syrup is a delicious sweet syrup, made with sugar and freshly squeezed lemon juice. It is used as a topping for beverages and desserts.
Serving: Makes ½ cup of syrup.
Preparation time: 5 minutes
Ready time: 20 minutes

Ingredients:
- 1/2 cup granulated sugar
- 1/2 cup freshly squeezed lemon juice
- 2 tablespoons butter (optional)
- Zest from 1 lemon

Instructions:
1. In a small saucepan, combine the sugar and lemon juice, and heat over medium heat, stirring constantly, until the sugar dissolves completely.
2. Bring the mixture to a boil, and then reduce the heat to a simmer.
3. Add the butter and lemon zest, stirring to combine.
4. Simmer for 15-20 minutes, stirring occasionally.
5. Remove from heat and allow to cool before using.

Nutrition information: Per 2 tablespoons of Lemon Syrup: Calories: 41, Total Fat: 1.3g, Saturated Fat: 0.7g, Cholesterol: 3mg, Sodium: 1.1mg, Total Carbohydrate: 11.1g, Dietary Fiber: 0.3g, Total Sugars: 11g, Protein: 0.0g.

14. Pineapple Syrup

This pineapple syrup is a sweet and fruity mixture of deliciousness! Enjoy it in any recipe or over ice cream for a sweet and delightful treat.
Serving: Makes 1/2 cup
Preparation time: 5 minutes
Ready time: 10 minutes

Ingredients:
- 1 cup of fresh pineapple, diced

- ¼ cup pineapple juice
- 1 tablespoon of cornstarch
- ½ cup sugar
- Pinch of salt

Instructions:
1. In a small saucepan, combine the diced pineapple, pineapple juice, cornstarch, sugar and salt.
2. Heat the mixture over medium-high heat, stirring constantly until it starts to thicken and bubble.
3. Reduce the heat to low and continue cooking for about 5 minutes, stirring occasionally, until thickened.
4. Remove from heat and let cool before serving.

Nutrition information:
Calories: 180 kcal, Carbohydrates:47 g, Protein:1 g, Fat:0 g, Sodium:45 mg, Sugars:42 g

15. Orange Syrup

Orange Syrup is a simple, delicious, and versatile topping for desserts or breakfast. It's made with only three Ingredients and is ready in just a few minutes.
Serving: Makes about 1 cup of syrup
Preparation time: 5 minutes
Ready time: 10 minutes

Ingredients:
- 2/3 cup freshly squeezed orange juice or strained orange juice
- 2/3 cup granulated sugar
- 2 tablespoons freshly grated orange zest

Instructions:
1. Place the orange juice, sugar, and orange zest in a small saucepan and stir to combine.
2. Bring to a boil over medium heat and cook, stirring occasionally, until the syrup thickens and turns a deep orange color, about 5 minutes.
3. Remove the syrup from the heat and let cool for about 5 minutes.

Nutrition information: Serving size- 2 tablespoons | Calories- 60 | Total fat- 0g | Sodium- 0mg | Total carbohydrate- 15g | Protein- 0g | Cholesterol- 0mg

16. Almond Syrup

Almond Syrup is a delicious syrup made from sweet almonds. It adds a great flavor and nutty sweetness to many cocktails, pastries, and desserts.
Serving: Makes 24 servings
Preparation Time: 10 minutes
Ready Time: 45 minutes

Ingredients:
• 2 cups of water
• 2 cups of sugar
• 2 teaspoons of almond extract

Instructions:
1. In a medium sauce pan, combine water and sugar.
2. Place the pan over medium heat and stir until the sugar is dissolved.
3. Add almond extract and bring the syrup to a low simmer.
4. Let the syrup simmer for about 30-45 minutes, stirring occasionally.
5. Once the syrup has reached the desired consistency, let it cool before serving.

Nutrition information:
Serving size: 1 tablespoon
Calories: 31
Fat: 0g
Carbohydrates: 8g
Protein: 0g

17. Hazelnut Syrup

Hazelnut Syrup is a sweet and nutty syrup that is easy to make and is perfect for adding to your coffee, pancakes or ice cream.

Serving: 4
Preparation Time: 10 minutes
Ready Time: 15 minutes

Ingredients:
- 2 tablespoons honey
- 2 cups of water
- 1 cup of hazelnuts, crushed
- 2 teaspoons of vanilla essence

Instructions:
1. Heat the 2 cups of water in a saucepan over medium heat.
2. Add the honey and the crushed hazelnuts and bring to a boil.
3. Simmer for 5 minutes, stirring occasionally.
4. Remove from heat and let cool before adding the vanilla essence.
5. Strain the mixture and store in a sterilized glass jar.

Nutrition information: per serving (4 servings): Calories: 84, Fat: 3g, Saturated Fat: 0.3g, Cholesterol: 0mg, Sodium: 2mg, Carbohydrates: 12g, Fiber: 2g, Sugar: 8g, Protein: 2g

18. Lavender Syrup

Lavender Syrup is an exquisite combination of fragrant lavender and sweet syrup, perfect on desserts or drinks.
Serving: 10-12 servings
Preparation Time: 5 minutes
Ready Time: 10 minutes

Ingredients:
• 2 cups of granulated sugar
• 1 cup of water
• 2 tablespoons of dried lavender
• A few drops of purple food coloring (optional)

Instructions:
1. In a medium-sized saucepan, add the sugar and water. Stir until completely combined and begin to heat over medium heat.

2. Once the mixture begins to simmer, add the lavender. Simmer for 10 minutes, stirring constantly.
3. Strain the mixture into a bowl and let cool.
4. Once cool, add a few drops of food coloring (if using).
5. Pour the mixture into a jar or bottle with a lid and store in the refrigerator.

Nutrition information: Each serving contains approximately 28.75 calories.

19. Mint Syrup

Mint syrup is a sweet, cooling condiment that adds a refreshing twist to a variety of foods. Perfect for topping ice cream or making your favorite soda or smoothie, this delicious syrup is easy to make with just a few Ingredients.
Serving: Makes 1 cup
Preparation Time: 10 minutes
Ready Time: 25 minutes

Ingredients:
- 2 cups water
- 2 cups sugar
- 1/2 cup loosely packed mint leaves

Instructions:
1. Place the water in a medium saucepan and heat it over medium-high heat until it is boiling.
2. Add in the sugar and stir until it is completely dissolved.
3. Remove the saucepan from the heat and add in the mint leaves. Let it steep for 15 minutes.
4. Strain the syrup through a fine-mesh sieve and discard the leaves.
5. Allow the syrup to cool before storing in an airtight container in the refrigerator.

Nutrition information: Per 1 tablespoon serving: 26 calories, 0 g fat, 7 g sugar

20. Ginger Syrup

Enjoy the sweet and spicy flavor of homemade ginger syrup with this simple recipe! Perfect for morning coffee, baking, and cocktails, this syrup is sure to tantalize your taste buds.
Serving: Makes 2 cups of syrup
Preparation Time: 10 minutes
Ready Time: 1 hour

Ingredients:
- 2 cups of water
- 2 cups of granulated sugar
- Half cup of freshly grated ginger
- 2 tablespoons vanilla extract

Instructions:
1. In a medium pot, add the water and sugar. Bring the mixture to a boil, stirring occasionally.
2. Once the mixture has begun to boil, reduce the heat to low and add the ginger. Simmer the syrup for 30 minutes.
3. After 30 minutes, stir in the vanilla extract and simmer for another 15 minutes.
4. Remove the syrup from heat and let it cool completely before transferring it to jars or bottles, for storage.

Nutrition information: Per serving (¼ cup): Calories 170, Total Fat 0g, Cholesterol 0mg, Sodium 0mg, Potassium 0g, Total Carbohydrates 45g, Dietary Fiber 0g, Sugars 43g, Protein 0g.

21. Honey Syrup

Honey Syrup is a popular simple syrup recipe to add sweetness and flavor to all types of drinks, cocktails and desserts.
Serving: Makes 1/2 cup of syrup
Preparation Time: 5 minutes
Ready Time: 5 minutes

Ingredients:
- 1/2 cup of honey
- 1/2 cup of water

Instructions:
1. In a small saucepan over medium-high heat, add honey and water.
2. Bring to a boil, stirring occasionally. Once boiling turn heat to low and simmer, stirring occasionally for 4-5 minutes.
3. Remove from heat and cool to room temperature.
4. Strain through a fine mesh strainer into a bowl and allow to cool completely.

Nutrition information:
Calories: 105, Fat: 0g, Carbohydrates: 28g, Protein: 0g, Sodium: 3mg

22. Espresso Syrup

Espresso syrup is a sweet syrup made of espresso, sugar, and vanilla. It has a concentrated espresso flavor with a hint of sweetness and can be used in many recipes or as a topping for desserts. It can also be used as a base for espresso-flavored cocktails, coffee drinks, and more.
Serving: Makes about 16 ounces of syrup
Preparation time: 15 minutes
Ready time: 1 hour

Ingredients:
- 4 shots of espresso
- 2 cups of water
- 2 cups of sugar
- 2 tablespoons of vanilla extract

Instructions:
1. In a large pot, combine the espresso shots and water. Bring to a boil over medium-high heat.
2. Reduce the heat to low and add the sugar. Stir until completely dissolved.
3. Remove from heat and add the vanilla extract. Stir to combine.

4. Allow the mixture to cool for about 10 minutes before transferring it to an airtight container.
5. Store in the refrigerator for up to 1 month.

Nutrition information:
Serving size: 1 tablespoon
Calories: 68
Total Fat: 0g
Total Carbohydrates: 15g
Sugar: 15g
Protein: 0g

23. Pomegranate Syrup

Pomegranate Syrup is a tart-sweet, naturally-colored syrup made from pomegranate juice and sugar. It can be used in a variety of recipes and marinades.
Serving: Makes 1 1/2 cups
Preparation Time : 5 minutes
Ready Time: 1 hour

Ingredients:
- 2 cups of pomegranate juice
- 1/2 cup of sugar

Instructions:
1. In a medium saucepan, combine the pomegranate juice and the sugar.
2. Bring it to a boil over medium-high heat, stirring constantly to dissolve the sugar.
3. Reduce the heat to low and simmer the mixture for about 30 minutes, or until it has reduced to about 1 1/2 cups.
4. Turn off the heat and let the syrup cool before transferring it to a container.

Nutrition information:
Pomegranate Syrup contains no fat and is a low-calorie sweetener. A 1/4 cup serving contains 120 calories, 32 g of carbohydrates, and 28 g of sugar.

24. Watermelon Syrup

Watermelon syrup is the perfect way to enjoy the sweet and refreshing flavor of watermelons. This easy-to-follow recipe will have you enjoying the deliciously sweet syrup in no time!
Serving: Makes one 12oz jar of syrup
Preparation time: 5 minutes
Ready time: 1 hour

Ingredients:
- 2 cups of fresh watermelon juice
- 2 cups of granulated sugar
- 1/4 teaspoon of citric acid

Instructions:
1. In a bowl, mix together the watermelon juice, sugar, and citric acid until combined.
2. Pour the mixture into a medium saucepan and bring it to a boil over medium heat.
3. Reduce the heat to low and let the mixture simmer for about 40 minutes or until the syrup thickens.
4. Once done, allow the syrup to cool down before transferring it into a 12oz jar. Store the syrup in the refrigerator for up to 2 weeks.

Nutrition information:
Calories: 332 kcal, Carbohydrates: 85 g, Protein: 0.3 g, Fat: 0.3 g, Sodium: 4 mg, Sugar: 82 g

25. Rose Syrup

Rose syrup is a deliciously sweet, classic syrup widely used in Middle Eastern cuisine. It is made using rose petals and sugar, and has an intensely floral aroma and flavor.
Serving: Makes approximately 1 1/4 cups
Preparation Time: 10 minutes
Ready Time: 4-6 hours

Ingredients:
3/4 cup rose petals
4 cups water
4 cups granulated sugar

Instructions:
1. In a medium saucepan over high heat, bring the water and rose petals to a boil.
2. Reduce the heat and simmer for about 5 minutes.
3. Add the sugar and stir until it has completely dissolved.
4. Keep stirring on low heat until the syrup has thickened (about 20 minutes).
5. Strain the syrup, pour it into a sterilized jar, and then let cool.
6. Keep in a sealed container in the refrigerator for up to a month.

Nutrition information: (per serving) Calories: 195 kcal, Carbohydrates: 49 g, Protein: 0.1 g, Fat: 0 g, Sodium: 0 g, Sugar: 65 g

26. Banana Syrup

Banana Syrup is sweet syrup made from boiled bananas, perfect for desserts, smoothies, and oatmeal.
Serving: Makes approximately 1-1/2 cups.
Preparation time: 10 minutes
Ready time: 45 minutes

Ingredients:
- 2-3 large ripe bananas, peeled
- 1/2 cup water
- 1/2 cup granulated sugar
- Pinch of salt

Instructions:
1. In a medium saucepan, mash the bananas with a potato masher.
2. Add the water, sugar, and salt, and bring to a boil over medium-high heat, stirring constantly.

3. Reduce heat to a simmer and cook for about 30-45 minutes, stirring occasionally, until the mixture thickens and reduces to 1-1/2 cups. The syrup should be thick enough to coat the back of a spoon.
4. Remove the syrup from the heat and let cool.

Nutrition information: Not available.

27. Mango Syrup

Sweet and fruity mango syrup is a great way to add flavor to any dish or snack. It can be used as a topping for pancakes and waffles, added to smoothies or mixed drinks, or cooked with meats and veggies.
Serving: Makes 1 quart
Preparation time: 5 minutes
Ready time: 2 hours

Ingredients:
- 3/4 cup of sugar
- 1/4 cup of water
- 2 cups of ripe mango, chopped
- 2 tablespoons of lemon juice
- 1/4 teaspoon of salt

Instructions:
1. In a medium saucepan, combine sugar and water and bring to a boil over medium-high heat.
2. Reduce heat to low and add mango. Cook for 10-15 minutes, stirring frequently.
3. Remove from heat and stir in lemon juice and salt.
4. Allow mixture to cool for 30 minutes, before blending until smooth.
5. Strain through a fine-mesh strainer, pressing gently on solids to extract as much liquid as possible.
6. Transfer to a bottle or jar and store in the refrigerator.

Nutrition information (per serving): 28 calories; 0.2 g fat; 6.2 g carbohydrates; 0.6 g protein; 0 mg cholesterol; 0.1 g sugar; 47 mg sodium.

28. Passion Fruit Syrup

Passion Fruit Syrup is a tangy and sweet syrup that is perfect for adding a little zest to your desserts and other culinary creations.
Serving: Makes 2 cups
Preparation time: 10 minutes
Ready time: 15 minutes

Ingredients:
2 cups passion fruit juice
1 cup honey

Instructions:
1. In a medium saucepan, combine the passion fruit juice with the honey.
2. Bring to a boil over medium-high heat, then reduce the heat to low and simmer for 5 minutes.
3. Remove from the heat and let cool completely.
4. Once cooled, pour the syrup into a container with a lid and store in the refrigerator for up to two weeks.

Nutrition information:
Nutrition Facts (per serving): Calories: 124, Fat: 0g, Carbohydrate: 32g, Protein: 0g

29. Pistachio Syrup

Pistachio Syrup is a delicious and easy-to-make sweet topping that can be used to enhance the flavor of many desserts. It is also a great topping for ice cream, pancakes, and waffles.
Serving: 12
Preparation time: 15 minutes
Ready time: 15 minutes

Ingredients:
- 2/3 cup shelled and chopped pistachios
- 1 cup granulated sugar
- 2 tablespoons honey

- 1/2 cup light corn syrup
- 1/2 teaspoon pure vanilla extract

Instructions:
1. In a medium saucepan, add the chopped pistachios, sugar, honey, light corn syrup and mix well.
2. Place the saucepan over medium heat and bring the mixture to a gentle boil.
3. Reduce the heat to low and simmer for 10 minutes, stirring occasionally.
4. Remove the saucepan from the heat and stir in the vanilla extract.
5. Allow the syrup to cool to room temperature.
6. Store the syrup in an airtight container for up to 2 weeks.

Nutrition information:
Per serving: 90 calories, 0g fat, 0mg cholesterol, 18g carbohydrates, 0g protein, 0mg sodium.

30. Cardamom Syrup

Cardamom Syrup is a delicious and versatile condiment that can be used to add a flavorful sweetness to absolutely anything - from coffee and cocktails, to desserts and snacks.
Serving: Makes approximately 1 3/4 cups
Preparation Time: 10 minutes
Ready Time: 15 minutes

Ingredients:
2 cups water
2 cups sugar
2 tablespoons ground cardamom

Instructions:
1. In a medium pot over medium-high heat, dissolve the sugar in the water, stirring until all of the sugar has dissolved.
2. Add in the ground cardamom and reduce the heat to low. Simmer for 5 minutes.
3. Remove from heat, cover and let it cool to room temperature.

4. Strain the cooled syrup through a fine mesh strainer lined with cheesecloth, discarding the solids.

Nutrition information: Per 2 tablespoons - 75 calories, 0 g fat, 20 mg sodium, 19 g carbohydrates, 19 g sugar

31. Elderflower Syrup

This easy-to-make Elderflower Syrup is a unique, sweet and aromatic syrup that can be used to sweeten a variety of drinks like lemonades, iced teas, smoothies, and homemade slushies.
Serving: 10
Preparation time: 20 minutes
Ready time: 8 to 24 hours

Ingredients:
 5 elderflower heads, 2 cups sugar, 2 cups water, 2 tablespoons freshly squeezed lemon juice

Instructions:
1. In a medium saucepan, combine the elderflower heads, sugar, water and lemon juice.
2. Bring the mixture to a rolling boil and then reduce to a simmer. Keep simmering for about 20 minutes.
3. Remove the mixture from the heat and allow it to cool down to room temperature.
4. Set a strainer over a pint-sized mason jar and strain the cooled syrup into the jar.
5. Screw the lid on the jar and store the elderflower syrup in the refrigerator.

Nutrition information: Serving size - 2 tablespoons (30ml). Calories - 100kcal, Total Fat - 0g, Sodium - 0mg, Total Carbohydrates - 26g, Sugars - 25g, Protein - 0g.

32. Cherry Blossom Syrup

This cherry blossom syrup is a delicious sweet syrup made from cherry blossom petals and sugar. It has a subtle floral flavor and can be added to many desserts to give them an extra special touch.

Serving: Yields 1 cup of syrup
Preparation time: 15 minutes
Ready time: 2 hours to overnight

Ingredients:
-2 cups of dried cherry blossom petals
-2 cups of sugar
-2 cups of water

Instructions:
1. Place cherry blossom petals in a medium pot.
2. Add sugar and water to the pot and stir until the sugar is dissolved.
3. Bring the mixture to a rolling boil and reduce the heat to a simmer.
4. Let the mixture simmer for about 20 minutes, stirring occasionally.
5. Strain the syrup through a fine mesh sieve into a bowl and discard the solids.
6. Allow the syrup to cool and transfer to a jar or bottle with an air-tight lid.
7. Refrigerate for 2 hours or overnight before serving.

Nutrition information: Per serving (1 cup): Calories--178, Fat--0g, Saturated fat--0g, Sodium--0mg, Carbohydrates--42g, Fiber--0g, Sugar--39g, Protein--0g

33. Hibiscus Syrup

This Hibiscus Syrup is a fragrant and flavorful syrup perfect as a topping for ice cream. The syrup is simple to make and can be kept for a few weeks in the refrigerator.

Serving: Makes about 1 cup
Preparation time: 10 mins
Ready time: 20-25 mins

Ingredients:
· 1 cup water

· 4-5 hibiscus flowers
· 1/2 cup sugar
· 1 tsp. Rose Water

Instructions:
1. Heat the water in a saucepan over medium heat, until it comes to a gentle boil.
2. Add the hibiscus flowers to the saucepan and reduce the heat slightly.
3. Simmer the hibiscus flowers in the water for 15 minutes, until the water turns a deep pink.
4. Remove the pan from the heat and stir in the sugar until fully dissolved.
5. Add the rose water to the syrup, stirring until blended.
6. Strain the syrup into a glass bowl and leave it to cool.

Nutrition information: Per serving, this syrup contains 39 calories, 0.7gm fat, 0.11gm saturates, 9.3gm carbohydrates, 0.12gm sodium, 0gm protein.

34. Pumpkin Spice Syrup

Pumpkin Spice Syrup adds a delicious layer of sweetness and flavor to many recipes. This rich and creamy syrup is perfect for topping pancakes, waffles, ice cream, and more!
Serving: 4
Preparation Time: 10 minutes
Ready Time: 25 minutes

Ingredients:
• 1 cup packed light-brown sugar
• 1/4 cup granulated sugar
• 1 cup pumpkin puree
• 3/4 cup heavy cream
• 2 tablespoons unsalted butter
• 1 teaspoon pure vanilla extract
• 1/2 teaspoon ground cinnamon
• 1/4 teaspoon ground ginger
• 1/4 teaspoon salt

Instructions:
1. In a medium saucepan set over medium heat, combine the sugars, pumpkin puree, heavy cream, butter, vanilla, cinnamon, ginger and salt.
2. Stir gently and bring the mixture to a boil. Once boiling, reduce the heat to low.
3. Simmer for 10 minutes, or until thickened and syrupy. Stir the mixture occasionally.
4. Place the syrup in an airtight container and store in the refrigerator for up to 1 week.

Nutrition information: Per serving (4 servings): Calories 209; Fat 8g; Cholesterol 32mg; Sodium 68mg; Carbohydrates 33g; Fiber 1g; Sugar 28g; Protein 2g.

35. Cranberry Syrup

Cranberry syrup is a delicious and tart condiment made with cranberries that can be used for a variety of recipes.
Serving: 4-6 servings
Preparation time: 15 minutes
Ready time: 25 minutes

Ingredients:
• 2 cups of fresh (or frozen) cranberries
• 2 cups of water
• 1 cup of sugar
• 1/4 teaspoon of ground cinnamon (optional)

Instructions:
1. Place the cranberries in a medium saucepan and add water
2. Simmer over medium-low heat for 10 minutes, stirring occasionally
3. Add the sugar and cinnamon and continue to simmer for another 5 minutes, stirring until the cranberries break up and the syrup thickens
4. Remove from heat and let cool, then strain into a jar or container
5. Serve with pancakes, ice cream, salads, or any recipe of your choice

Nutrition information:

1 serving of cranberry syrup (1/4 cup) contains approximately 70 calories, 18 g of sugar, and 0.5 g of fat.

36. Guava Syrup

Guava syrup is a delightful tropical twist to your favorite recipes and beverages. It is easy to make and offers a sweet and unique flavor to your recipes. Serve it over ice cream, pancakes, waffles, and more!
Serving: Up to 8
Preparation time: 10 minutes
Ready time: 20 minutes

Ingredients:
- 3 large guavas, peeled and de-seeded
- 1 cup of white sugar
- 2 cups of water

Instructions:
1. In a medium saucepan, bring the sugar and water to a boil over medium-high heat
2. Reduce heat to a simmer and add the guava pieces
3. Simmer the mixture for 10 minutes, stirring occasionally
4. Remove from the heat and allow the guava syrup to cool slightly
5. Pour the mixture through a strainer lined with a cheesecloth and discard the solids
6. Transfer the guava syrup to an airtight container and store it in the refrigerator

Nutrition information:
Calories: 50, Fat: 0g, Cholesterol: 0mg, sodium: 0mg, Carbohydrates: 13g, Protein: 0g, Fiber: 0g

37. Kiwi Syrup

This Kiwi Syrup is a delicious and easy to make syrup you can use to drizzle over fruits, pancakes, waffles, and other desserts.
Serving: Makes about 1 cup

Preparation Time: 10 minutes
Ready Time: 20 minutes

Ingredients:
-2 large kiwis, peeled
-1 cup of water
-2 tablespoons of fresh lemon juice
-1/2 cup of sugar

Instructions:
1. In a blender, add the kiwis, water, and lemon juice. Blend until it becomes a smooth puree.
2. Pour the contents of the blender into a medium pot and add the sugar.
3. Place the pot over medium heat and stir until the sugar has dissolved.
4. Bring the mix to a boil and allow it to simmer for about 10 minutes, stirring occasionally.
5. Remove the pot from the heat and let it cool completely.
6. Store the cooled syrup in an airtight container in the refrigerator and use within one week.

Nutrition information: 91cal; 0 fat; 22.8g sugar; 0g protein; 24.6g carbs; 0.1g fiber; 10.1mg sodium

38. Tangerine Syrup

Tangerine Syrup is an incredibly simple and versatile recipe that can be used for both sweet and savory dishes. It has a bright and citrusy flavor that can be used to enhance cocktails, marinades, stir-frys, and desserts.
Serving: Makes 12 servings
Preparation time: 5 minutes
Ready time: 20 minutes

Ingredients:
• 1/2 cup of cane sugar
• 1/2 cup of tangerine juice
• 2 tablespoons of freshly grated tangerine zest
• 2 cups of orange blossom water

Instructions:
1. In a medium saucepan, heat up the sugar on medium heat and let it melt.
2. Stir in the tangerine juice and zest.
3. Once the mixture is boiling, reduce heat to a simmer.
4. Let the syrup cook for 15 minutes until it has thickened.
5. Remove from the heat and stir in the orange blossom water.
6. Let the syrup cool before transferring into a glass jar with an airtight lid.

Nutrition information:
• Calories: 40 kcal
• Fat: 0 g
• Carbohydrates: 10 g
• Protein: 0 g

·39. Butterscotch Syrup

Butterscotch syrup is a rich, flavorful syrup made with brown sugar, butter, and cream. It is a delicious choice for desserts, cakes, pancakes, waffles, ice cream, and many more.
Serving: Makes 1/2 cup
Preparation Time: 5 minutes
Ready time: 10 minutes

Ingredients:
• 1/2 cup light brown sugar, packed
• 2 tablespoons butter
• 2 tablespoons light corn syrup
• Pinch of salt
• 2 tablespoons heavy cream

Instructions:
1. In a medium saucepan, combine the brown sugar, butter, corn syrup, and salt.
2. Heat over medium heat, stirring constantly, until the butter is melted and the sugar is dissolved.

3. Increase the heat to medium-high and continue to cook, stirring occasionally, for 5 minutes.
4. Remove from heat and stir in the cream.
5. Set aside to cool slightly before serving.

Nutrition information: Per serving: Calories 90; Fat 3.5 g; Carbohydrate 15 g; Protein 0 g; Sodium 16 mg; Sugar 12 g.

40. Grape Syrup

Grape Syrup is a deliciously sweet syrup made from fresh red grapes. The syrup is great for drizzling over breakfasts and desserts, or for adding some flavor to marinades and sauces.
Serving: Makes about 5 cups of syrup
Preparation Time: 8 hours
Ready Time: 8 hours

Ingredients:
- 5 pounds of red grapes
- 2 tablespoons of lemon juice
- 2 cups of light brown sugar
- 2 cinnamon sticks

Instructions:
1. Wash the grapes thoroughly to remove any dirt or debris.
2. Place the grapes in a large pot and bring to a boil over medium-high heat.
3. Once boiling, reduce the heat and simmer for 1-2 hours.
4. Once the grapes are soft, mash them using a potato masher or immersion blender.
5. Add the lemon juice and sugar and simmer over medium heat for another 1-2 hours, stirring occasionally.
6. Add the cinnamon sticks and simmer for an additional 30 minutes.
7. Strain the mixture through a fine sieve to remove any solids.
8. Pour the syrup into clean bottles or jars and seal. The syrup can be refrigerated for up to 2 weeks.

Nutrition information:

Calories: 182
Total Fat: 0.2g
Saturated Fat: 0.1g
Cholesterol: 0mg
Sodium: 7mg
Carbohydrates: 48g
Fiber: 1.8g
Sugar: 46.7g
Protein: 1.2g

41. Fig Syrup

Enjoy the rich taste of figs with this easy-to-make syrup. It is perfect for topping ice cream, pancakes, waffles, muffins, toast, and more.
Serving: One cup.
Preparation Time: 10 minutes
Ready Time: 30 minutes

Ingredients:
- 2 cups fresh figs, stems removed
- 1 cup of water
- 2 teaspoons of lemon juice
- 2 tablespoons of honey (optional)

Instructions:
1. In a medium saucepan over medium heat, bring the figs and water to a gentle simmer. Allow the mixture to simmer, stirring occasionally, for 25-30 minutes.
2. Remove the saucepan from heat and stir in the lemon juice and honey (optional).
3. Allow the mixture to cool slightly then transfer it to a food processor, blender, or immersion blender and blend until desired consistency is reached.
4. Pour the syrup into a jar or bottle and store it in the refrigerator for up to two weeks.

Nutrition information:

Serving size: one cup, Calories: 60, Fat: 0g, Carbohydrate: 14g, Protein: 1g, Sugar 14g, Sodium: 5mg.

42. Cinnamon Syrup

Cinnamon Syrup is a delicious, aromatic syrup that can be used to enhance the flavor of coffee, cakes, smoothies, and more.
Serving: Makes 2 cups syrup
Preparation Time: 5 minutes
Ready Time: 10 minutes

Ingredients:
• 2 cups granulated sugar
• 1 cup water
• 2 cinnamon sticks
• 1 teaspoon ground cinnamon

Instructions:
1. In a saucepan, bring the sugar and water to a boil over high heat.
2. Reduce the heat to low and add the cinnamon sticks and ground cinnamon. Stir to combine.
3. Simmer for 4-5 minutes or until the sugar is dissolved and the syrup has thickened.
4. Remove the cinnamon sticks.
5. Ladle the mixture into a glass jar and allow to cool.

Nutrition information: Serving size: 1/4 cup, Calories: 124, Saturated fat: 0g, Sodium: 1mg, Total carbohydrates: 33g, Sugars: 33g

43. Irish Cream Syrup

Irish Cream Syrup is a delicious, creamy syrup made of Irish cream liqueur and other syrups. It makes an excellent topping for desserts and coffee or can be served on ice cream and crepes, mixing wonderful flavors together.
Serving: 4-6

Preparation Time: 5 minutes
Ready Time: 5 minutes

Ingredients:
- 3/4 cup Irish Cream liqueur
- 1/4 cup light corn syrup
- 1/4 cup dark corn syrup

Instructions:
1. In a medium saucepan, combine Irish cream liqueur, light and dark corn syrups.
2. Cook over medium heat, stirring constantly, until mixture is thick and bubbly.
3. Reduce heat and simmer for 1-2 minutes.
4. Remove from heat and cool completely before serving.

Nutrition information:
Calories: 126 kcal, Carbohydrates: 15.7 g, Protein: 0.3 g, Fat: 0 g, Saturated Fat: 0 g, Cholesterol: 0 mg, Sodium: 2 mg, Potassium: 20 mg, Sugar: 14.7 g, Vitamin A: 0%, Vitamin C: 0%, Calcium: 1%, Iron: 1%

44. Salted Caramel Syrup

This delicious Salted Caramel Syrup recipe will have your tastebuds dancing with its combination of salty and sweet flavors!
Serving: Makes 10 Servings
Preparation time: 10 minutes
Ready time: 10 minutes

Ingredients:
• 1 cup of light brown sugar
• ½ cup of heavy cream
• 3 tablespoons of butter
• 1 tablespoon of sea salt
• 1 ½ teaspoons of vanilla extract

Instructions:

1. In a medium saucepan, melt the butter and brown sugar over medium heat until fully combined.
2. Slowly add in the heavy cream, whisking continuously until smooth.
3. Allow the mixture to come to a boil, whisking continuously for 2 minutes.
4. Remove the saucepan from the heat and stir in the sea salt and vanilla extract.
5. Allow the syrup to cool and then pour it into a bottle or jar with a lid.

Nutrition information
Serving size: Approx. 2 tablespoons
Calories: 166, Fat: 8 g, Carbohydrates: 20 g, Protein: 0 g

45. Pear Syrup

Pear Syrup is a naturally sweet and flavorful condiment that's the perfect match for everything from sweet pancakes to savory main dishes. It's quick and easy to make at home with a few simple ingredients.
Serving: Makes 1 1/2 cups
Preparation Time: 10 minutes
Ready Time: 30 minutes

Ingredients:
 3 cups diced pears, 1/2 cup honey, 2 tablespoons lemon juice, 1/4 teaspoon cinnamon

Instructions:
1. In a medium saucepan, combine the diced pears, honey, lemon juice, and cinnamon.
2. Bring to a low boil, stirring frequently.
3. Reduce heat to low and simmer for 15-20 minutes, stirring occasionally, until pears become very soft and begin to break apart.
4. Remove from heat and allow to cool slightly.
5. Purée the syrup in a blender until completely smooth.
6. Strain the syrup through a fine-mesh strainer to remove any chunks and small pieces of pears.
7. Pour into a glass jar and store in the fridge for up to two weeks.

Nutrition information: Calories: 91, Total Fat: 0g, Sodium: 2mg, Potassium: 91mg, Carbohydrates: 24g, Fiber: 1g, Sugar: 21g, Protein: 0g

46. Apricot Syrup

Apricot Syrup is a golden syrup made from simmered apricots that is used as a topping or spread. It also adds an additional layer of flavor to desserts and tea.
Serving: 2 servings
Preparation Time: 10 minutes
Ready Time: 20 minutes

Ingredients:
- 10 apricots
- 1 cup of sugar
- 1 teaspoon of cornstarch
- 2 tablespoons of water

Instructions:
1. Cut the apricots in half and scoop out the pits. Place the apricots in a blender and pulse them until they form a puree.
2. Pour the pureed apricots into a medium-sized saucepan and place it over medium heat.
3. Add the sugar and stir the mixture until the sugar dissolves.
4. In a small bowl, mix the cornstarch and water together and then add it to the apricot mixture.
5. Raise the heat of the mixture to high and bring it to a boil.
6. Boil the mixture for about 10 minutes, stirring it often.
7. Once it is done boiling, transfer the syrup to a glass jar or bowl and let it cool.

Nutrition information: per Serving:
- Calories: 150
- Total Fat: 0.2g
- Cholesterol: 0mg
- Sodium: 8mg
- Protein: 1.6g

- Total Carbs: 36g
- Dietary Fiber: 2g

47. Rosemary Syrup

Rosemary Syrup is an easy-to-make syrup that is fragrant and sweet.
Perfect for adding as a topping to pancakes, waffles, and other desserts.
Serving: Makes about 1 cup of syrup
Preparation Time: 5 minutes
Ready Time: 10 minutes

Ingredients:
- 1 cup water
- 2/3 cup granulated sugar
- 2 sprigs of fresh rosemary

Instructions:
1. In a small saucepan over medium heat, bring the water to a boil.
2. Add in the sugar and rosemary and stir until the sugar is dissolved.
3. Reduce the heat to low and let the mixture simmer for 5 minutes.
4. Remove from heat and strain the syrup to remove the rosemary.
5. Let the syrup cool and store in an airtight container in the refrigerator.

Nutrition information: A 1 tablespoon serving size of Rosemary Syrup contains 50 calories, 12 g of sugar and 0 g of fat.

48. Coconut Lime Syrup

This delicious Coconut Lime Syrup is the perfect addition to any dessert.
It has a subtle sweet taste with a hint of lime, while the coconut adds an extra tropical flavor dimension to the syrup.
Serving: This recipe makes 2 cups and serves about 8.
Preparation time: Prep time is 5 minutes.
Ready time: Ready in 30 minutes.

Ingredients:
• 2 cups coconut sugar

- 1/2 cup freshly squeezed lime juice
- Pinch of salt
- 2 tablespoons lime zest

Instructions:
1. In a large bowl, mix together the coconut sugar, lime juice, and salt.
2. Add the lime zest and mix together until evenly combined.
3. Pour the mixture into a small saucepan and bring to a slow simmer.
4. Let gently simmer for about 15 minutes, stirring occasionally.
5. After the mixture has thickened, remove from heat and let cool for 10 minutes.
6. Transfer the coconut lime syrup to an airtight container and store in the refrigerator.

Nutrition information
Serving size: 2 tablespoons
Calories: 50
Total fat: 0 g
Total carbohydrate: 12 g
Sugar: 10 g
Sodium: 0 mg

49. White Chocolate Syrup

White Chocolate Syrup is a delicious and simple topping for all kinds of desserts or ice cream toppings. Made with just a few simple Ingredients, this syrup is perfect for all occasions and all ages.
Serving: Makes about 10 to 12 servings
Preparation time: 5 minutes
Ready time: 10 minutes

Ingredients:
- 2/3 cup white chocolate chips
- 2/3 cup sweetened condensed milk
- 2 tablespoons light corn syrup

Instructions:

1. In a medium-sized, non-stick saucepan, over medium heat, combine the white chocolate chips and sweetened condensed milk. Stir continuously until chips melt and mixture thickens, about 5 minutes.
2. Remove from heat and stir in light corn syrup.
3. Let cool to room temperature.
4. Serve over ice cream, pancakes, waffles, pastries or fruit.

Nutrition information:
Calories: 119, Total Fat: 5.9 g, Saturated Fat: 3.5 g, Cholesterol: 17 mg, Carbohydrates: 14.5 g, Protein: 2.2 g, Sodium: 30 mg

50. Gingerbread Syrup

Make the sweet and spicy flavors of your favorite holiday dessert any time with this recipe for Gingerbread Syrup.
Serving: Makes about 1 1/2 cups of Gingerbread Syrup
Preparation time: 10 minutes
Ready time: 15 minutes

Ingredients:
• 2 cups granulated sugar
• 1 cup light-brown sugar
• 1/2 cup molasses
• 1 cup water
• 2 cinnamon sticks
• 1 teaspoon ground ginger
• 1/4 teaspoon ground cloves
• 1/4 teaspoon ground nutmeg
• Juice of 1 lemon

Instructions:
1. Place all of the Ingredients in a medium saucepan over medium-high heat.
2. Stir continuously until the sugar is dissolved and the syrup starts to boil.
3. Immediately reduce to a simmer and stir occasionally for 5 minutes.
4. Place a fine-mesh sieve over a bowl and strain the syrup, discarding the solids. Cool before using.

Nutrition information:
Calories: 354 kcal, Carbohydrates: 94 g, Protein: 0 g, Fat: 0 g, Saturated Fat: 0 g, Sodium: 47 mg, Potassium: 410 mg, Fiber: 0 g, Sugar: 87 g, Vitamin A: 95 IU, Vitamin C: 1 mg, Calcium: 98 mg, Iron: 2 mg

51. Blueberry Lemon Syrup

Blueberry Lemon Syrup is a sweet and tangy syrup where ripe blueberries and lemons are cooked together to make a flavorful syrup for a variety of breakfast and dessert dishes.
Serving: Makes 2 pints
Preparation time: 10 minutes
Ready time: 20 minutes

Ingredients:
- 4 cups fresh or frozen blueberries
- 1/3 cup sugar
- 1/2 cup freshly-squeezed lemon juice

Instructions:
1. Place the blueberries and sugar in a medium saucepan over medium-high heat. Cook, stirring often, until the berries break down and release their juices, about 10 minutes.
2. Stir in the lemon juice and bring the mixture to a boil. Reduce the heat and simmer for 10 minutes, or until the mixture is thick and syrupy.
3. Remove from the heat and let cool before bottling the syrup in air-tight containers.

Nutrition information:
Calories: 138 kcal, Carbohydrates: 36 g, Protein: 1 g, Sugar: 30 g, Sodium: 4mg, Fiber: 2 g

52. Mint Chocolate Syrup

Mint Chocolate Syrup is a delicious treat that combines the cooling flavor of mint with the sweetness of chocolate. It's perfect for stirring into coffee, milkshakes, and other drinks, and is easily made at home.
Serving: Serves 8
Preparation time: 5 minutes
Ready time: 10 minutes

Ingredients:

• 3/4 cup sugar
• 3/4 cup cocoa powder
• 2/3 cup water
• 2 teaspoons peppermint extract

Instructions:
1. In a medium saucepan, combine the sugar, cocoa powder, and water. Stir to combine.
2. Bring the mixture to a boil over medium-high heat, stirring constantly.
3. Reduce the heat to low and simmer for 5 minutes, stirring frequently.
4. Remove from the heat and stir in the peppermint extract.
5. Let cool for a few minutes before serving.

Nutrition information per serving: Calories 120, Fat 0.5g, Sodium 0.6mg, Carbohydrate 26g, Protein 0.6g

53. Blackcurrant Syrup

Blackcurrant syrup is a sweet syrup made from blackcurrants. It can be enjoyed in a variety of ways such as over ice cream and pancakes, added to cocktails and mocktails, or used as a condiment.
Serving: Approximately 1/4 cup (60 mL)
Preparation time: 5-7 minutes
Ready time: 2 hours

Ingredients:
- 2 cups (500 mL) fresh blackcurrants
- 1/2 cup (180 g) sugar
- 1/2 cup (125 mL) water

Instructions:
1. Wash and stem the blackcurrants.
2. In a small saucepan, combine the sugar and water. Simmer over medium-high heat until the sugar has dissolved, stirring occasionally.
3. Add the blackcurrants to the syrup and simmer for 5-7 minutes.
4. Remove from heat, then strain the mixture through a sieve, pressing with a wooden spoon to extract as much liquid as possible.
5. Allow the syrup to cool, then transfer it to a jar or bottle with a lid.
6. Refrigerate for a minimum of two hours before using.

Nutrition information (Per Serving): Calories: 100, Sugars: 13 g, Sodium: 0 mg

54. Praline Syrup

Praline syrup is a rich, creamy, and delicious topping that makes a great addition to a variety of desserts, pancakes, ice cream sundae and milkshakes.
Serving: 4
Preparation Time: 5 minutes
Ready Time: 15 minutes

Ingredients:
- 1/2 cup packed light brown sugar
- 1/4 cup butter
- 1/3 cup heavy cream
- 1 teaspoon vanilla extract
- 1/4 cup chopped pecans

Instructions:
1. In a medium saucepan over medium heat, melt butter, stirring in brown sugar.
2. Add heavy cream and stir until sugar has dissolved.
3. Add vanilla extract and stir until combined.
4. Bring to a low boil and cook for about 5 minutes, stirring often.
5. Remove from heat and stir in chopped pecans.
6. Let cool for 10 minutes.

7. Store in an air-tight container and refrigerate for up to a week.

Nutrition information: Per Serving: Calories 295, Total Fat 21.1g, Cholesterol 53mg, Sodium 98mg, Total Carbohydrate 25.2g, Protein 2.6g.

55. Blood Orange Syrup

This Blood Orange Syrup is a sweet and tart condiment that is full of fruity and zesty flavor. It's perfect for adding a splash of exotic flavor to breakfast, cocktails, and desserts.
Serving: 4
Preparation time: 10 minutes
Ready time: 20 minutes

Ingredients:
• 2 cups of blood orange juice (from about 4-5 blood oranges)
• 1 cup of white sugar
• 2 tablespoons of freshly squeezed lemon juice
• 1 teaspoon of orange zest

Instructions:
1. In a saucepan, add the sugar and blood orange juice and stir until the sugar is completely dissolved.
2. Add the lemon juice and orange zest and stir.
3. Simmer over medium-high heat until the syrup has been reduced by half, about 10 minutes.
4. Strain the syrup through a fine-mesh strainer and discard the zest.
5. Store in an airtight container and refrigerate until ready to use.

Nutrition information:
• Calories: 136
• Carbohydrates: 34 g
• Protein: 0.5 g
• Fat: 0 g
• Sodium: 2 mg

56. Toasted Marshmallow Syrup

This Toasted Marshmallow Syrup is an easy and delicious homemade syrup. It takes just minutes to make and adds the perfect amount of sweetness to your favorite coffee, tea, smoothies, and desserts.
Serving: Makes 1.5 cups
Preparation time: 5 minutes
Ready time: 10 minutes

Ingredients:
- 2 cups of sugar
- 1/2 cup water
- 1 teaspoon of vanilla extract
- 1 tablespoon of butter
- 1 teaspoon of light corn syrup
- 1/2 teaspoon of kosher salt

Instructions:
1. In a medium saucepan, combine the sugar, water, vanilla extract, butter, light corn syrup, and salt.
2. Place the saucepan over medium heat and mix together, stirring constantly until the sugar is dissolved.
3. Increase the heat to high and bring the mixture to a boil. Boil for 3-4 minutes or until the syrup starts to thicken and become golden yellow in color.
4. Reduce the heat to medium-low and carefully pour in the marshmallows. Stir constantly until the marshmallows have melted and are fully integrated into the syrup.
5. Remove the toasted marshmallow syrup from the heat and let cool.

Nutrition information: Serving size - 1 tablespoon; Calories - 50; Fat - 0g; Cholesterol - 0mg; Sodium - 15mg; Carbohydrates - 12g; Protein - 0g.

57. Cherry Vanilla Syrup

This Cherry Vanilla Syrup is a delicious and fruity topping for pancakes, waffles, crepes and other breakfast favorites! It's also great on top of ice cream, oatmeal and desserts.
Serving: Makes 3/4 cup syrup
Preparation Time: 5 minutes
Ready time: 5 minutes

Ingredients:
1½ cups frozen dark sweet cherries, thawed
1½ cup granulated sugar
½ teaspoon pure vanilla extract

Instructions:
1. Place cherries, sugar and 1/3 cup water in a medium saucepan over medium-high heat. Bring mixture to a boil, stirring constantly.
2. Reduce heat to low and simmer, stirring constantly, until the cherries are softened and liquid has thickened, about 3-5 minutes.
3. Remove from heat and stir in vanilla extract.
4. Serve warm over plain or vanilla yogurt, vanilla ice cream, pancakes, waffles or oatmeal.

Nutrition information: Serving size: 2 tablespoons, Calories: 70, Total Fat: 0g, Cholesterol: 0mg, Sodium: 0mg, Total Carbohydrates: 18g, Protein: 0g

58. Lychee Syrup

Lychee syrup is a sweet syrup made from pureed lychee fruit, which adds a subtle and sweet flavor to both drinks and desserts.
Serving: Makes about 3 cups
Preparation time: 15 minutes
Ready time: 15 minutes

Ingredients:
- 2 cups lychee puree
- 1 cup granulated sugar
- Juice of 2 lemons

Instructions:
1. In a medium pot over medium heat, add the lychee puree, sugar, and lemon juice.
2. Bring the entire mixture to a gentle simmer, stirring it frequently to dissolve the sugar.
3. Reduce the heat, and continue to simmer gently for 10 minutes.
4. Strain the syrup through a fine mesh sieve, discarding the seeds and pulp.
5. Allow the syrup to cool at room temperature before transferring it to a jar or bottle.

Nutrition information: Per serving of 2 tbsp – (81g): Calories 107, Total fat 0.2g, Saturated fat 0.1g, Trans fat 0g, Cholesterol 0mg, Sodium 3mg, Total Carbohydrate 27.8g, Dietary Fiber 0g, Total Sugars 27.5g, Protein 0.1g.

59. Raspberry Lime Syrup

Raspberry Lime Syrup is a refreshing sweet syrup that adds a delicious flavor to pancakes, waffles, oatmeal, and even ice cream.
Serving: Makes one and quarter cups (310ml).
Preparation time: 5 minutes.
Ready time: 10 minutes.

Ingredients:
• 1 cup (185g) fresh raspberries
• 2/3 cup (150g) sugar
• 1/3 cup (80ml) lime or lemon juice
• 2 teaspoon lime zest

Instructions:
1. In a medium saucepan, add the raspberries, sugar, lime or lemon juice.
2. Heat over medium heat for approximately 5 minutes while stirring constantly.
3. Reduce the heat to low and continue stirring until the syrup has thickened.
4. Remove from the heat and stir in the lime zest.
5. Allow to cool before serving.

Nutrition information: 135 calories, Carbohydrates 34g, Sugars 34g, Protein 1g, Fat 0g, Sodium 1mg

60. Earl Grey Syrup

Earl Grey Syrup is a unique and simple syrup that is made with black tea. With an intoxicating aroma and robust flavor, this syrup is perfect for making espresso, lemonades, iced tea, cocktails, and other drinks.
Serving: Makes 4 servings
Preparation Time: 10 minutes
Ready Time: 25 minutes

Ingredients:
1 cup sugar
1 cup water
3 Earl Grey tea bags

Instructions:
1. In a medium saucepan, add the sugar and water and bring to a boil.
2. Reduce heat to a low and add three Earl Grey tea bags.
3. Simmer mixture for 15 minutes, stirring occasionally.
4. Remove syrup from heat and let steep for 10 minutes.
5. Strain syrup and discard tea bags. Let syrup cool.

Nutrition information (per serving):
Calories: 60
Protein: 0 g
Fat: 0 g
Carbohydrates: 15 g

61. Pumpkin Caramel Syrup

This Pumpkin Caramel Syrup is a deliciously rich and sweet recipe with a perfect blend of spiced pumpkin and creamy caramel. It's an easy to make syrup that can be used to add an extra layer of sweetness and flavor on your favorite snacks.

Serving: 8
Preparation time: 10 minutes
Ready time: 10 minutes

Ingredients:
- 2 cups granulated sugar
- 2 tablespoons pumpkin pie spice
- ½ cup heavy cream
- 1 teaspoon vanilla extract
- ½ cup canned pumpkin puree

Instructions:
1. In a medium saucepan, combine sugar, pumpkin pie spice, heavy cream and vanilla extract.
2. Heat over medium heat, stirring until sugar melts and mixture is well combined.
3. Add in the pumpkin puree and continue stirring until mixture is combined.
4. Reduce heat to low and simmer for 8 minutes.
5. Remove from heat and let cool before pouring into a clean container.

Nutrition information: Per serving: 218 calories; 6.7 g fat; 0.7 g protein; 40.5 g carbohydrates; 0 g fiber; 44 mg sodium.

62. Saffron Syrup

Sweet and exotic, saffron syrup is truly a unique treat for the taste buds! It's made with simple Ingredients but has an extraordinary flavor.
Serving: 4
Preparation Time: 10 minutes
Ready Time: 1 hour

Ingredients:
- 1/4 cup water
- 1/4 cup sugar
- 1/4 teaspoon ground saffron
- 2 tablespoons honey
- 1/4 teaspoon ground cardamom

Instructions:

1. In a small saucepan, combine the water, sugar, saffron, honey, and cardamom.
2. Heat over medium-low heat and whisk until the sugar is dissolved, about 10 minutes.
3. Increase heat to medium and let simmer until the syrup thickens and starts to coat the back of a spoon, about 15 minutes.
4. Pour into a glass jar, let cool to room temperature, and store in the refrigerator for up to 1 month.

Nutrition information:

- 208 calories
- 0 g fat
- 56 g carbohydrates
- 0 g protein
- 1 mg sodium

63. Kiwi Strawberry Syrup

Kiwi Strawberry Syrup is a delicious way to add a refreshing and tangy flavor to your meal! With a few ingredients, you can make this easy and delicious syrup to top off anything from cakes to pancakes!
Serving: 8
Preparation time: 5 minutes
Ready time: 10 minutes

Ingredients:

2 kiwis, 2 cups strawberries; cut, 1/2 cup white sugar, 1 cup water

Instructions:

1. In a medium-sized saucepan, combine the kiwis, strawberries, sugar, and water.
2. Heat the mixture over medium-high heat stirring occasionally until the sugar is fully dissolved and the mixture is boiling.
3. Reduce to a low heat and simmer for 5 minutes. There should be a syrupy consistency.
4. Remove from heat and let cool before transferring to a jar.

Nutrition information: 111 calories per serving, 0.1g fat, 28g carbohydrates, 0.5g protein

64. Apple Pie Syrup

Apple Pie Syrup is a delicious topping for pancakes, waffles, and more. This versatile syrup makes a great addition to any breakfast item or a topping for a slice of freshly baked apple pie.
Serving: Makes 4-6 servings
Preparation time: 5 minutes
Ready time: 10 minutes

Ingredients:
- 2 teaspoons ground cinnamon
- ¾ cup light brown sugar
- 2 tablespoons cornstarch
- ¼ teaspoon sea salt
- 2 cups apple cider
- 2 tablespoons butter
- 2 teaspoons pure vanilla extract

Instructions:
1. In a medium pot, combine the cinnamon, brown sugar, cornstarch, and salt.
2. Pour in the apple cider and stir until there are no lumps.
3. Place over medium heat and bring to a low boil; stirring continuously until the mixture thickens, about 5 minutes.
4. Add in the butter and vanilla extract and stir until the butter melts.
5. Remove from heat and transfer to a jar for storage.

Nutrition information: Calories: 115, Total Fat: 3.5g, Saturated Fat: 2g, Cholesterol: 10mg, Sodium: 100mg, Total Carbohydrates: 18g, Dietary Fiber: 0.5g, Sugars: 10g, Protein: 0.2g

65. Salted Caramel Mocha Syrup

Creamy, sweet, and salty, Salted Caramel Mocha Syrup is sure to satisfy any sweet tooth. This delicious syrup is great to put over ice cream, waffles, pancakes, or coffee.
Serving: Makes 4 servings
Preparation Time: 10 minutes
Ready Time: 30 minutes

Ingredients:
- 2 cups sugar
- 2/3 cup water
- 1/2 cup light corn syrup
- 1/4 cup cocoa powder
- 2 tablespoons brewed espresso
- 2 tablespoons coconut oil
- 2 teaspoons caramel extract
- 1 teaspoon salt

Instructions:
1. In a medium saucepan, combine the sugar, water, corn syrup, cocoa powder, and brewed espresso.
2. Heat the mixture over medium-high heat until it begins to boil.
3. Reduce the heat and simmer for 15 minutes, stirring occasionally.
4. Remove the saucepan from the heat and stir in the coconut oil, caramel extract, and salt until combined.
5. Allow the syrup to cool to room temperature before serving.

Nutrition information: per serving - Calories: 415, Fat: 1.6g, Carbohydrates: 104g, Protein: 0.3g, Fiber: 0.8g

66. Maple Pecan Syrup

Maple Pecan Syrup is a flavorful and delicious topping perfect for waffles, ice cream or pancakes.
Serving: 4
Preparation time: 10 minutes
Ready time: 10 minutes

Ingredients:

- 1/3 cup of pecans
- 1/3 cup of maple syrup
- 2 tablespoons of sugar
- 2 tablespoons of butter
- A pinch of cinnamon

Instructions:

1. Preheat your oven to 350 degrees.
2. In a small baking dish, spread the pecan pieces in an even layer.
3. Bake for 8-10 minutes, or until the pieces are lightly toasted.
4. In a medium saucepan, melt the butter over medium heat.
5. Add the maple syrup, sugar, and cinnamon and bring to a simmer.
6. Stir in the toasted pecans and simmer for 2 minutes.
7. Remove from heat and pour the syrup into a bowl. Let cool for 5 minutes.
8. Serve warm over your favorite desserts.

Nutrition information: Serving size: 1, Calories: 160, Fat: 9g, Saturated fat: 4g, Cholesterol: 15mg, Sodium: 45mg, Carbohydrates: 19g, Fiber: 1g, Sugar: 16g, Protein: 1g.

67. Brown Sugar Syrup

Brown Sugar Syrup is a simple and delicious syrup made with three simple Ingredients - brown sugar, water, and lemon juice. The syrup adds sweetness and depth of flavor to pancakes, waffles, and French toast.
Serving: Serves 4
Preparation time: 10 minutes
Ready time: 10 minutes

Ingredients:
-1 cup brown sugar
-1/2 cup water
-1 tablespoon freshly squeezed lemon juice

Instructions:

1. In a medium saucepan over medium heat, combine the brown sugar and water.

2. Bring to a simmer, stirring often, until the sugar dissolves completely.
3. Remove from the heat and stir in the lemon juice.
4. Let cool for 5 minutes.
5. Transfer to a jar or airtight container and store in the refrigerator for up to 2 weeks.

Nutrition information:
Per Serving: Calories: 162 kcal, Carbohydrates: 43 g, Protein: 0 g, Fat: 0 g, Saturated Fat: 0 g, Sodium: 2 mg, Fiber: 0 g, Sugar: 43 g

68. Passionfruit Mango Syrup

Take your mango and passion fruit syrup to the next level with this mouth-watering recipe! It's incredibly easy to make and adds a wonderful tropical flavor to your favorite dishes.
Serving: 4-6
Preparation time: 10 minutes
Ready time: 45 minutes

Ingredients:
• 2 passion fruits
• 2 large mangos, peeled and pureed
• 1 cup white sugar
• 1 ½ cup water
• Lemon juice (optional)

Instructions:
1. Remove the pulp from the passion fruits and place them in a blender.
2. Add the mango puree, sugar, and water to the blender. Blend until smooth.
3. Strain the mixture to remove any chunks.
4. Pour the mixture into a saucepan and heat it over medium-high heat for about 10 minutes.
5. Reduce the heat to low and cook for about 30 minutes, stirring occasionally.
6. Remove the syrup from the heat and cool. Add a dash of lemon juice if desired.

Nutrition information: Per 1-tablespoon serving (about 4-6 servings): Calories: 25, Fat: 0g, Saturated fat: 0g, Carbohydrates: 6.5g, Sugar: 6g, Sodium: 0mg, Fiber: 0g, Protein: 0g

69. Rosewater Syrup

Rosewater Syrup is a popular syrup recipe popularly used in Middle Eastern and North African cuisines. This syrup is easy to make, and adds a delicious floral and flavorful taste to drinks and desserts.
Serving: 4
Preparation Time: 10 minutes
Ready Time: 10 minutes

Ingredients:
• 2 cups Water
• 2 cups White Sugar
• 1 teaspoon Rosewater

Instructions:
1. In a small saucepan, mix together the water and sugar.
2. Heat the mixture over medium-high heat and bring to a boil.
3. Once boiling, reduce the heat to low and let simmer for 5 minutes.
4. After 5 minutes have passed, add in the rosewater and stir to combine.
5. Simmer for an additional 3-5 minutes.
6. Turn off the heat and let the syrup cool before using.

Nutrition information: per serving - 224 calories, 0 g fat, 57 g carbohydrates, 0 g protein

70. Ginger Lemongrass Syrup

Ginger Lemongrass Syrup is a delicious syrup that can be added to beverages and other desserts for an extra special flavor. This recipe is easy to make and delicious.
Serving: Makes about 2 cups of syrup
Preparation time: 15 minutes
Ready time: 30 minutes

Ingredients:
- 2 cups white sugar
- 4 lemongrass stalks, chopped and crushed
- 2 cups hot water
- 2" piece ginger, peeled and chopped

Instructions:
1. In a small saucepan over medium heat, combine sugar, lemongrass, and hot water. Stir until the sugar is dissolved.
2. Reduce the heat to low and add the ginger. Simmer for 15 minutes, stirring occasionally.
3. Strain the liquid through a fine-mesh sieve and discard the solids.
4. Transfer the syrup to a mason jar or heat-proof container and let cool to room temperature.
5. Store in the refrigerator for up to two weeks.

Nutrition information
Per serving (1/4 cup): 149 calories; 0.5 g fat; 0 g saturated fat; 37 g carbohydrates; 0 g protein; 0 mg sodium; 0 g fiber

71. Pineapple Coconut Syrup

This sweet and simple syrup is a combination of tropical flavors that is sure to make any dessert stand out.
Serving: Makes 8 servings
Preparation Time: 10 minutes
Ready Time: 1 hour 10 minutes

Ingredients:
- 1 cup sugar
- ¼ cup light corn syrup
- 1 cup water
- 1 teaspoon almond extract
- 1 cup crushed pineapple
- ¾ cup coconut flakes

Instructions:

1. In a medium saucepan, mix together the sugar and corn syrup, then add the water.
2. Bring the mixture to a boil, stirring constantly, and reduce heat to a simmer.
3. Once the sugar has dissolved, stir in the almond extract, crushed pineapple, and coconut flakes.
4. Simmer the mixture for approximately 45 minutes, until thickened, stirring occasionally.
5. Once thickened, pour into a clean jar or container and allow to cool.

Nutrition information: Per Serving- Calories: 151, Fat: 3g, Saturated Fat: 2g, Cholesterol: 0mg, Sodium: 4mg, Carbohydrates: 30g, Fiber: 1g, Sugar: 17g, Protein: 1g.

72. Pistachio Rose Syrup

Enjoy decadent flavor with a hint of rose with this Pistachio Rose Syrup recipe. This delightful syrup is perfect for topping cakes, waffles, pancakes and ice cream.
Serving: 6 servings
Preparation Time: 10 minutes
Ready Time: 10 minutes

Ingredients:
- 1/2 cup granulated sugar
- 1/2 cup water
- 1 teaspoon rose water
- 1/2 cup pistachios, shelled and coarsely chopped
- Pinch of nutmeg

Instructions:
1. Place a medium saucepan over medium heat and add the sugar and water. Stir until sugar is dissolved and let the mixture come to a boil.
2. Add in the rose water, pistachios and nutmeg. Reduce the heat and let it simmer for about 5 minutes.
3. Remove from heat and use a fine-mesh strainer to discard the solids.
4. Pour the syrup into a bottle or jar and store in the refrigerator for up to 2 weeks.

Nutrition information: per serving (2 tablespoons): Calories 104.8, Carbohydrates 13.9g, Protein 1.4 g, Fat 4.1g

73. Honey Lavender Syrup

Honey Lavender Syrup is a wonderfully fragrant and flavorful syrup that can be used for a variety of culinary applications.
Serving: Makes 2 1/2 cups
Preparation Time: 5 minutes
Ready Time: 25 minutes

Ingredients:
- 2 1/2 cups water
- 1/4 cup culinary-grade dried lavender
- 1 1/2 cups granulated sugar
- 1/2 cup honey

Instructions:
1. In a medium saucepan, bring the water to a boil.
2. Add the lavender, stir, and reduce the heat to medium-low.
3. Simmer for 10 minutes.
4. Strain the lavender from the water and discard the lavender.
5. Return the lavender-flavored water to the saucepan over medium heat.
6. Add the sugar and stir until it's dissolved.
7. Stir in the honey and bring the mixture to a boil.
8. Reduce the heat to low and simmer for 10 minutes.
9. Remove from the heat and let cool completely before transferring to a sterilized glass container.

Nutrition information:
-Calories: 104
-Total Fat: 0g
-Sodium: 2mg
-Total Carbohydrates: 27g
-Protein: 0.3g

74. Raspberry White Chocolate Syrup

Raspberry White Chocolate Syrup is a sweet and creamy topping that's perfect for ice cream, pancakes, and other desserts. It's an indulgent and delightful treat the whole family will enjoy.
Serving: 6
Preparation Time: 10 minutes
Ready Time: 30 minutes

Ingredients:
- 1/2 cup heavy cream
- 1/2 cup white chocolate chips
- 1/3 cup plus 2 tablespoons sugar
- 1 cup frozen raspberries
- 2 tablespoon butter

Instructions:
1. In a small saucepan, combine the heavy cream, white chocolate chips, and sugar.
2. Cook over medium heat, stirring occasionally, until the white chocolate chips are melted and the mixture is smooth.
3. Add the frozen raspberries and butter to the pan.
4. Cook for 8-10 minutes, stirring occasionally, until the raspberries are soft and the syrup has thickened.
5. Remove from heat and let cool before using.

Nutrition information:
Calories: 241, Fat: 14.3g, Carbohydrates: 25.9g, Protein: 2.8g, Sodium: 44mg, Fiber: 2.9g

75. Blood Orange Elderflower Syrup

Blood Orange Elderflower Syrup is a sweet and tangy syrup made with colors and fragrances of the season. With its bright hue, this syrup is perfect for topping pancakes, waffles, French toast, and more!
Serving: 5-7
Preparation Time: 10 minutes
Ready Time: 1 hour

Ingredients:
- 2 1/2 cups fresh blood oranges, peeled and cut into segments
- 1/4 cup honey
- 2 tablespoons elderflower liqueur
- 2 teaspoons of freshly squeezed lemon juice
- 1/2 teaspoon of sea salt

Instructions:
1. In a medium saucepan, combine the blood orange segments, honey, elderflower liqueur, lemon juice, and sea salt.
2. Bring the mixture to a boil over medium-high heat, stirring occasionally to dissolve the honey.
3. Once the mixture has reached a boil, reduce the heat to low and allow the syrup to simmer for 20-30 minutes until it thickens slightly.
4. Remove the syrup from the heat and allow it to cool before serving.

Nutrition information:
- Calories: 90
- Total Fat: 0.5g
- Sodium: 70mg
- Carbohydrates: 22g
- Fiber: 0g
- Sugar: 17g

76. Maple Bacon Syrup

Enjoy the decadent and savory combination of maple and bacon in a delicious syrup with Maple Bacon Syrup. This could be used over pancakes, French toast, oatmeal, and more for a creative and tasty addition to your breakfast.
Serving: Up to 10 servings.
Preparation Time: 10 minutes.
Ready Time: 25 minutes.

Ingredients:
- 6 slices bacon
- 1/2 cup maple syrup

- 1/4 teaspoon ground black pepper
- 1/4 teaspoon garlic powder
- 1/2 teaspoon onion powder

Instructions:
1. Preheat the oven to 375 degrees Fahrenheit. Place the bacon strips onto a baking sheet and bake for 12-15 minutes, or until crispy.
2. Remove the bacon from the oven and let cool. Chop into small pieces.
3. Place the maple syrup, pepper, garlic powder, and onion powder into a small saucepan. On medium-low heat, bring the syrup to a light simmer and cook for 5 minutes.
4. Add in the bacon pieces and cook for an additional 5 minutes.
5. Remove the syrup from the heat when done and let cool for 10 minutes.

Nutrition information: Per Serving: Calories: 94, Total Fat: 4.8g, Saturated Fat: 1.9g, Trans Fat: 0g, Cholesterol: 12mg, Sodium: 95mg, Carbohydrates: 9g, Fiber: 0g, Sugar: 9g, Protein: 3.2g

77. Amaretto Syrup

Amaretto Syrup is a delicious and simple recipe made with basic Ingredients and a lot of flavor. It's perfect for topping ice cream, adding to coffees and storing in the fridge.
Serving: Makes about 1½ cups syrup
Preparation Time: 5 minutes
Ready Time: 10 minutes

Ingredients:
-1 cup white sugar
-1 cup water
-1 teaspoon almond extract

Instructions:
1. In a small saucepan, combine the white sugar and water. Bring it to a boil over medium-high heat.
2. Once boiling, reduce the heat to low and let it simmer for 5 minutes, stirring occasionally.

3. Remove from heat, stir in the almond extract, and let it cool.
4. Store the syrup in a jar or airtight container in the refrigerator for up to 2 weeks.

Nutrition information: Per 2 tablespoons (109 grams) serving: calories 111, total fat 0 g, saturated fat 0 g, cholesterol 0 mg, sodium 0 mg, potassium 0 mg, total carbohydrates 28 g, dietary fiber 0 g, sugars 28 g, protein 0 g.

78. Chai Spice Syrup

Chai Spice Syrup is a thick, sweet syrup perfect for adding hints of spice to your favorite drinks. Its robust flavor will bring warmth and complexity to your beverages.
Serving: Makes about 3/4 cup
Preparation Time: 5 minutes
Ready Time: 10 minutes

Ingredients:
• 1 cup water
• 1 cup granulated sugar
• 2 star anise pods
• 2 cinnamon sticks
• 1 teaspoon ground ginger
• 2 cardamom pods
• 2-3 whole cloves
• 1 teaspoon black peppercorns
• 1 teaspoon vanilla extract
• ¾ cup light brown sugar

Instructions:
1. In a small saucepan over medium-high heat, combine the water and granulated sugar and mix until the sugar is dissolved.
2. Add in the star anise, cinnamon sticks, ground ginger, cardamom pods, whole cloves and peppercorns and bring to a boil.
3. Reduce the heat to low and simmer for about 5 minutes, stirring occasionally.

4. Remove from heat and add in the vanilla extract and light brown sugar and stir until combined.
5. Let cool for a few minutes and strain the spices.
6. Transfer the syrup to an airtight container and store in the refrigerator for up to three weeks.

Nutrition information:
Calories: 204
Fat: 0g
Carbohydrates: 52.5g
Protein: 0g

79. Cherry Limeade Syrup

This refreshing syrup will bring a delightful zing to your summer beverages! It only takes a few minutes to make and features a tart cherry limeade flavor that everyone is sure to love.
Serving: Makes 1 ½ cups
Preparation time: 5 minutes
Ready time: 5 minutes

Ingredients:
- 2 cups granulated sugar
- ½ cup water
- 1 ½ cups fresh lime juice
- 1 1/4 cups tart cherry juice
- 1 teaspoon lime zest
- 1 teaspoon tart cherry extract

Instructions:
1. In a small saucepan, combine the sugar and water and bring to a gentle boil over medium-high heat.
2. Once boiling, reduce the heat to low and add the lime juice, cherry juice, lime zest, and cherry extract.
3. Simmer for 3-4 minutes, or until the liquid reduces to a syrup consistency.
4. Remove from heat and let cool before transferring to an airtight container.

Nutrition information: per tbsp. - 45 calories, 0g fat, 11g carbohydrates, 0g protein

80. Fig Vanilla Syrup

Fig Vanilla Syrup is a delightful treat that provides an amazing combination of sweet and tart with a hint of sweetness from the Fig and Vanilla flavors. This syrup can be used to top a variety of desserts, pancakes, or toast.
Serving: Makes 4 servings
Preparation Time: 10 minutes
Ready Time: 15 minutes

Ingredients:
- ½ cup diced dried figs
- ¾ cup of maple syrup
- 1 teaspoon of vanilla bean paste (or 1 teaspoon of pure vanilla extract)

Instructions:
1. In a small saucepan, heat the maple syrup over medium-high heat.
2. Add in the diced dried figs and stir until all the Ingredients are combined.
3. Reduce the heat to low and simmer for 10 minutes.
4. Add in the vanilla bean paste (or pure vanilla extract) and stir to combine.
5. Increase the heat to medium and simmer for an additional 5 minutes.
6. Remove from heat and allow the syrup to cool and thicken.
7. After the syrup has completely cooled, strain to remove the figs.
8. Serve over your favorite dessert or pancakes.

Nutrition information: Calories: 101, Fat: 0g, Carbs: 25g, Protein: 0g, Sugar: 21g

81. Blackberry Mint Syrup

This quick and airy Blackberry Mint Syrup is a surprisingly delightful addition to breakfast, brunch, or a sweet topping for your favorite desserts.
Serving - 2 cups
Preparation Time - 5 minutes
Ready Time - 10 minutes

Ingredients:
- 2 cups fresh blackberries
- 1 cup granulated sugar
- ½ cup water
- 1 sprig fresh mint leaves

Instructions:
1. In a medium saucepan over medium heat, combine blackberries, sugar, and water. Mash the blackberries with a potato masher and stir, bringing the mixture to a simmer.
2. Add the mint leaves and simmer for 8-10 minutes, stirring occasionally. The syrup should be thick and syrupy.
3. Remove from heat and strain into a heatproof bowl. Discard the solids. Let the syrup cool to room temperature.
4. Serve as a topping over yogurt, pancakes, waffles, ice cream, or desserts.

Nutrition information
Per serving (2 tablespoons): Calories - 38, Total fat - 0g, Cholesterol - 0mg, Sodium - 0mg, Carbohydrates - 10g, Fiber - 1g, Sugar - 8g, Protein - 0g.

82. Lemon Blueberry Syrup

This Lemon Blueberry Syrup is the perfect topping to your favorite pancakes or waffles! Sweet, tangy, and with just a hint of tartness, the syrup will definitely bring life to your morning breakfast and is sure to please everyone.
Serving: 4-6 people
Preparation Time: 10 minutes
Ready Time: 10 minutes

Ingredients:
- 2 cups fresh blueberries
- 1/2 cup freshly squeezed lemon juice
- 1/2 cup white sugar
- 1/4 cup water
- 2 tablespoons cornstarch

Instructions:
1. In a medium saucepan over medium heat, add the blueberries, lemon juice, sugar, and water. Bring to a low simmer, stirring often.
2. In a small bowl, mix the cornstarch with 2 tablespoons of cold water and stir until completely dissolved.
3. Once the blueberries are softened, add in the cornstarch mixture and stir. Allow the syrup to simmer for about 5 minutes or until the desired thickness is reached.
4. Serve over waffles or pancakes and enjoy!

Nutrition information:
- Calories: 105 kcal
- Carbohydrates: 27 g
- Protein: 0 g
- Fat: 0 g
- Sodium: 0 mg
- Potassium: 67 mg
- Fiber: 1 g
- Sugar: 25 g

83. Ginger Plum Syrup

Ginger Plum Syrup is a simple and delicious recipe that is the perfect addition to any breakfast or brunch. This syrup is made with fresh plums and ginger and is a great way to inject some natural sweetness to any meal.
Serving: Serves 4
Preparation time: 10 minutes
Ready time: 15 minutes

Ingredients:
- 2 cups pitted and chopped plums
- ¼ cup fresh ginger, peeled and chopped
- ½ cup honey or maple syrup
- ½ teaspoon ground cinnamon
- ½ cup water

Instructions:
1. Put the plums, ginger, honey or syrup, and cinnamon into a saucepan.
2. Add the water and bring to a low simmer over medium heat.
3. Allow the syrup to simmer for 10 minutes, stirring occasionally.
4. Turn off the heat and let the mixture cool.
5. Strain the syrup through a fine mesh sieve to remove the solids.
6. Store the syrup in a glass container for up to two weeks.

Nutrition information
Each serving contains approximately 80 calories, 1g fat, 20g sugar, 1g protein, and 2g fiber.

84. Caramel Macchiato Syrup

Caramel macchiato syrup is an easy and delicious way to bring a smooth, creamy taste to anything from your morning latte to a delicious ice cream sundae. This recipe makes a syrup with a rich, buttery caramel flavor that adds a special flair to whatever you intend to use it on.
Serving: 12 ounces
Preparation Time: 10 minutes
Ready Time: 10 minutes

Ingredients:
- 1/2 cup butter - 1/2 cup white sugar - 1/2 cup brown sugar - 1 cup light corn syrup - 1/4 teaspoon salt - 1 teaspoon vanilla extract

Instructions:
1. In a medium saucepan over medium-high heat, combine butter, white sugar, brown sugar, corn syrup, and salt.
2. Bring to a boil, stirring constantly. Once boiling, reduce heat slightly and simmer for 3 minutes, stirring frequently.

3. Remove from heat and stir in the vanilla extract.
4. Allow to cool for 5 minutes before using.

Nutrition information: Per serving, this syrup contains 180 calories, 7g of fat, 28g of carbohydrates, and 0g of protein.

85. Raspberry Hibiscus Syrup

This Raspberry Hibiscus Syrup is a sweet and tangy syrup that can be used to brighten up smoothies, cocktails, and desserts.
Serving: Makes 12 ounces syrup
Preparation Time: 10 minutes
Ready time: 15 minutes

Ingredients:
- 2 cups fresh or frozen raspberries
- 1/2 cup dried hibiscus flowers
- 2 1/4 cups of water
- 2 cups of white sugar

Instructions:
1.In a medium saucepan, bring 2 ¼ cups of water to a boil over medium-high heat.
2. Add 2 cups of white sugar and stir until sugar has dissolved.
3. Reduce heat to low and add the raspberries and hibiscus flowers. Simmer for 10 minutes.
4. Use a fine-mesh sieve or cheesecloth to strain the mixture into a heat-proof bowl, and let cool before transferring to a sterilized jar or bottle.

Nutrition information: Not available.

86. Lavender Vanilla Syrup

Lavender Vanilla Syrup is a delightful flavor combination of fragrant lavender and warm vanilla that is perfect for creating healthy and delicious drinks and desserts.
Serving: Makes 16 servings

Preparation time: 10 minutes
Ready time: 30 minutes

Ingredients:
- ⅔ cup Dried lavender
- 2 cups Filtered water
- 2½ cups Sugar
- 1½ teaspoons Pure vanilla extract

Instructions:
1. In a medium saucepan over medium heat, combine lavender and water. Bring to a gentle simmer, and then reduce heat to low. Simmer for 25 minutes.
2. Add the sugar and stir until it has completely dissolved.
3. Remove from heat and allow to cool for 5 minutes.
4. Strain the mixture into a clean container and discard the lavender. Add the vanilla extract to the syrup.

Nutrition information: 16 servings of Lavender Vanilla Syrup, each containing about 60 calories, 0.25 g of fat, 16.25 g of carbohydrates, and 0 g of protein.

87. Coconut Pineapple Syrup

Sweet and tart Coconut Pineapple Syrup is a flavorful way to top your favorite pancakes, waffles, and crepes! Serving: Makes 2 1/2 cups Preparation time: 5 minutes Ready time: 25 minutes

Ingredients:
- 2 cups coconut milk
- 2 cups coconut sugar
- 2 tablespoons cornstarch
- 1 cup fresh pineapple, diced
- 1 tablespoon freshly squeezed lemon juice

Instructions:
1. In a medium saucepan, whisk together the coconut milk, coconut sugar, and cornstarch over medium-high heat.

2. Bring to a gentle boil, stirring constantly.
3. Reduce the heat to medium and simmer for about 15 minutes, until the syrup is thick and coats the back of a spoon.
4. Stir in the pineapple and lemon juice and simmer for an additional 5 minutes.
5. Remove from the heat and let cool.
6. Serve on pancakes, waffles, or crepes.

Nutrition information: Serving size: 2 tablespoons | Servings per container: 17 | Calories per serving: 101 | Total fat: 1g | Saturated fat: 1g | Total carbohydrates: 20g | Dietary fiber: 1g | Sugars: 18g | Protein: 1g

88. Pistachio Cardamom Syrup

Pistachio Cardamom Syrup is an aromatic and flavorful syrup perfect for use in coffee, over pancakes, or in cocktails. This recipe yields approximately 1 cup of syrup.
Serving: 1 cup
Preparation Time: 10 minutes
Ready Time: 1 hour

Ingredients:
- 1 cup of water
- 2 Ha' tsp of cardamom seed, crushed lightly
- 2 cups of white sugar
- ¾ cup of shelled, unsalted pistachios

Instructions:
1. Put the crushed cardamom seeds and the water in a medium saucepan and let them steep for around 10 minutes.
2. Add the sugar to the saucepan and bring the mixture to a boil while stirring, for about 1 minute, or until the sugar is dissolved.
3. Add the pistachios to the pan and reduce the heat to a simmer. Cook for around 10 minutes, stirring regularly.
4. Strain the syrup through a fine mesh strainer to get rid of the solids.
5. Let the syrup cool for at least 30 minutes, stirring occasionally.

6. Once cooled, transfer the syrup to an air-tight container and store in the refrigerator.

Nutrition information:
Calories: 80
Total Fat: 0g
Cholesterol: 0mg
Sodium: 1mg
Carbohydrates: 20g
Protein: 1g

89. Mango Passionfruit Syrup

This recipe provides instructions on how to make a delicious and refreshing mango passionfruit syrup. It is perfect to top on desserts, yogurt, or pancakes.
Serving: Makes about 1 cup
Preparation time: 10 minutes
Ready time: 10 minutes

Ingredients:
- 2 cups ripe mango, peeled and diced
- ½ cup passionfruit juice
- ¼ cup honey or agave syrup

Instructions:
1. In a medium bowl, mash the mango and stir in passionfruit juice.
2. Strain the mixture and add the honey or agave syrup. Mix until all Ingredients are fully incorporated.
3. Bring the mixture to a boil, reduce heat and let simmer for 5 minutes.
4. Remove from heat, pour the syrup into a jar and let cool before serving.

Nutrition information: A serving of mango passionfruit syrup contains 59 calories, 15g of carbohydrates, 12g of sugars, 0g fat, 0g of protein.

90. Praline Pecan Syrup

Praline Pecan Syrup is an easy and delicious syrup recipe made with toasted pecans and brown sugar. It is ideal for topping waffles, ice cream, or pancakes, and it is sure to be a hit with friends and family.
Serving: Makes 1 cup
Preparation time: 15 mins
Ready time: 40 mins

Ingredients:
- 2 cups pecans
- 2/3 cup unsalted butter
- 1 cup light brown sugar
- 1 teaspoon pure vanilla extract

Instructions:
1. Preheat oven to 350° F (175° C).
2. Spread pecans in a single layer on a baking sheet and bake for 8 minutes, until lightly toasted. Allow to cool.
3. In a medium saucepan, heat butter and brown sugar over medium heat. Stir constantly until butter is melted and sugar is dissolved.
4. Bring mixture to a light boil. Boil for two minutes, stirring continuously.
5. Remove from heat and add toasted pecans and vanilla extract, stirring to combine.
6. Allow pecan syrup to cool for 20-30 minutes.

Nutrition information:
Per serving: Calories 391; Fat 27.1g; Cholesterol 32.9mg; Sodium 45.1mg; Carbohydrates 38.5g; Fiber 2.7g; Protein 3.2g.

91. Blackberry Sage Syrup

Make this easy and flavorful blackberry sage syrup to be enjoyed over your favorite pancakes, waffles, French toasts and more.
Serving: Makes 3 cups
Preparation time: 10 minutes
Ready time: 25 minutes

Ingredients:
- 2 cups blackberries, fresh or frozen
- ½ cup honey
- 2 cups water
- 10 fresh sage leaves

Instructions:
1. In a medium saucepan, add blackberries, honey, and water.
2. Bring to a simmer and cook for about 15 minutes, stirring occasionally.
3. Add in the sage leaves and simmer for an additional 5 minutes.
4. Take off the heat and use a potato masher to mash the blackberries in the syrup.
5. Strain the syrup into a gallon jar or decanter.
6. Let the syrup cool before using.

Nutrition information:
Per 2 tablespoons: 40 calories, 0g fat, 10g carbohydrates, 7g sugar, 1g protein.

92. Maple Walnut Syrup

Maple Walnut Syrup is a sweet, nutty, delicious syrup that can be used over many different desserts or as a topping for pancakes and waffles.
Serving: 8-10
Preparation Time: 10 minutes
Ready Time: 30 minutes

Ingredients:
- 2 cups pure maple syrup
- 1/2 cup chopped walnuts

Instructions:
1. Combine maple syrup and walnuts in a medium saucepan.
2. Cook over medium heat and bring to a boil, stirring occasionally.
3. Reduce heat to low and simmer for 20 minutes.
4. Allow mixture to cool before serving.

Nutrition information:
Calories – 186, Total Fat – 7g, Saturated Fat – 1g, Cholesterol – 0mg, Sodium – 2mg, Total Carbohydrate – 28g, Dietary Fiber – 1g, Sugars – 26g, Protein – 2g

93. Brown Butter Syrup

Brown butter syrup is a unique and delicious frosting, dip, and glaze that adds a rich, nutty flavor to any dish. It is simple to make and a great way to put a new spin on some of your old favorite recipes.
Serving: 4-6
Preparation time: 5 minutes
Ready time: 10 minutes

Ingredients:
• 3 tablespoons unsalted butter
• 2 tablespoons light brown sugar
• 1/2 teaspoon ground cinnamon • 2 teaspoons pure maple syrup

Instructions:
1. In a small saucepan, melt the butter on medium heat until lightly browned and fragrant, about 2 minutes.
2. Add the brown sugar, cinnamon, and maple syrup to the pan and bring to a simmer.
3. Cook, stirring constantly, until the mixture thickens, about 3 minutes.
4. Remove from heat and let cool slightly.

Nutrition information:
Calories: 98 | Carbohydrates: 12g | Fat: 6g | Protein: 0g | Sodium: 20mg | Sugar: 11g

94. Peach Ginger Syrup

This Peach Ginger Syrup is a yummy treat that's easy to whip up and full of sweetness and warmth. It's perfect for topping pancakes, waffles, oatmeal, ice cream, and everyday desserts.

Serving: Makes about 2 cups of syrup.
Preparation time: 10 minutes
Ready time: 20 minutes

Ingredients:
- 2 cups freshly cut peaches
- ½ cup sugar
- ½ cup water
- 1 teaspoon fresh ginger, minced

Instructions:
1. Combine all the Ingredients in a medium saucepan.
2. Bring to a gentle boil over medium heat, stirring occasionally.
3. Reduce the heat slightly and allow to simmer uncovered for 15-20 minutes, stirring occasionally.
4. Remove from heat and let cool slightly before serving.

Nutrition information:
Calories: 119 | Carbohydrates: 30g | Sodium: 1mg | Sugar: 28g

95. Cherry Almond Syrup

Cherry Almond Syrup is a sweet and tart syrup made from cherries and almond extract with a hint of honey. It's perfect for topping ice cream, waffles, and French toast.
Serving: Makes 1 cup
Preparation Time: 10 minutes
Ready Time: 15 minutes

Ingredients:
- 1½ cups frozen, pitted cherries
- 1 cup water
- ¼ cup honey
- 2 teaspoons almond extract
- 2 teaspoons cornstarch

Instructions:

1. In a small saucepan, combine cherries, water, honey, and almond extract over medium-high heat. Bring to a simmer and cook for 8 minutes, stirring occasionally.
2. In a small bowl, dissolve cornstarch in 2 tablespoons of water.
3. Pour the cornstarch mixture into the saucepan and stir to combine. Simmer for an additional 2 minutes, stirring constantly, until thickened.
4. Remove from heat and strain syrup through a mesh strainer into a bowl.

Nutrition information:
Serving Size: 1 Tablespoon
Calories – 20
Total Fat – 0 g
Sodium – 0 mg
Total Carbohydrate – 5 g
Protein – 0 g

96. Lemon Ginger Syrup

Lemon Ginger Syrup is a sweet and tangy syrup perfect for topping pancakes, ice cream and more. It's palate-pleasing for children and adults alike.
Serving: Makes 4 servings.
Preparation time: 10 minutes
Ready time: 15 minutes

Ingredients:
• 1 cup brown sugar
• 1 cup water
• 2 tablespoons fresh ginger, minced
• 1/2 cup fresh lemon juice
• 1/4 teaspoon ground nutmeg

Instructions:
1. In a medium pot over medium-high heat, combine the brown sugar and water and stir until the sugar has dissolved.
2. Add the minced ginger and bring the mixture to a boil.
3. Reduce heat to low and simmer for 5 minutes, stirring occasionally.

4. Remove from heat and stir in the lemon juice and nutmeg.
5. Cool completely before serving.

Nutrition information: Per 1/4 cup serving: calories – 100, fat – 0g, carbohydrate – 25g, protein – 0g, sodium – 3mg.

97. Raspberry Rose Syrup

Raspberry Rose Syrup is a delicious fruity syrup with a light floral flavor. It is perfect for topping pancakes, ice cream, cakes, waffles, and more! Enjoy the unique flavor combination of raspberries and roses with this simple and easy recipe.
Serving: Makes about 1 3/4 cups
Preparation Time: 10 minutes
Ready Time: 1 hour

Ingredients:
- 2 cups fresh raspberries
- 1/2 cup granulated sugar
- 1 teaspoon rose extract
- 1/4 teaspoon salt

Instructions:
1. In a medium saucepan, combine the raspberries, sugar, rose extract and salt.
2. Bring the mixture to a low boil, reduce the heat and simmer for 10 minutes.
3. Remove from heat and allow to cool.
4. Transfer the mixture to a blender or food processor and blend until smooth.
5. Return the mixture to the pan and simmer for an additional 20-25 minutes until the syrup thickens.
6. Remove from heat and allow to cool.
7. Pour the syrup into a sealable container and store in the refrigerator for up to 1 month.

Nutrition information: per 2-tablespoon serving: Calories 40, Fat 0g, Sodium 65mg, Carbohydrates 10g, Protein 0g.

98. Pineapple Mango Syrup

Pineapple Mango Syrup is a refreshing tropical-inspired mixture of sweet citrusy and mellow fruit flavors that makes a great topping for pancakes, waffles, and more! Serve up this delicious syrup for a truly unique breakfast experience.

Serving: 4-6
Preparation Time: 10 minutes
Ready Time: 15 minutes

Ingredients:
• 2 pineapples, peeled and chopped
• 2 mangos, peeled and chopped
• 1/3 cup sugar
• 1 tablespoon lemon juice
• 1/2 teaspoon ground ginger

Instructions:
1. In a blender, blend the pineapple and mango until smooth.
2. Transfer the mixture to a saucepan and add the sugar and lemon juice. Stir to combine.
3. Bring the mixture to a boil over medium-high heat, stirring occasionally.
4. Reduce the heat to low and simmer for 10 minutes, stirring occasionally.
5. Remove from heat and stir in the ground ginger.
6. Allow the syrup to cool before serving.
7. Serve over pancakes, waffles, or ice cream.

Nutrition information: Per serving (4-6 servings): Calories: 159, Total Fat: 0g, Cholesterol: 0mg, Sodium: 1mg, Total Carbohydrates: 41g, Protein: 1g.

99. Pistachio Almond Syrup

Pistachio Almond Syrup is an easy and delicious topping for everything from pancakes to ice cream. It has a sweet and nutty flavor that will make your desserts come alive with flavor. This recipe is full of flavor, nutrition, and sweetness that will delight your guests.

Serving: 6
Preparation Time: 10 minutes
Ready Time: 10 minutes

Ingredients:
- ¾ cup salted pistachios
- ¾ cup slivered almonds
- 1 cup of water
- ¼ cup white sugar
- ½ teaspoon almond extract
- ¼ teaspoon sea salt

Instructions:
1. Preheat oven to 350°F and line a baking sheet with parchment paper.
2. Spread the pistachios and slivered almonds in a single layer on the baking sheet.
3. Toast the nuts for 8-10 minutes, stirring halfway through. Remove from oven and let cool.
4. Place the cooled pistachios and almonds into a blender and blend until desired consistency is reached.
5. In a small saucepan, heat the water, sugar, almond extract, and salt until sugar dissolves.
6. Remove from heat and stir in the nut mixture.
7. Pour the mixture into a glass jar and let cool completely before sealing.

Nutrition information: Per serving: Calories: 122, Fat 6g, Sodium: 104mg, Carbohydrate: 14g, Fiber: 2g, Protein: 3g

100. Apple Caramel Syrup

This delicious Apple Caramel Syrup recipe is perfect for adding a touch of sweetness and a subtle apple flavor to drinks and desserts. The perfect balance of tart apple and rich caramel results in an irresistible syrup!
Serving: Makes about 1 ½ cups

Preparation Time: 10 minutes
Ready Time: 30 minutes

Ingredients:
- 2/3 cup chopped tart apples
- 1/4 cup butter
- 2/3 cup light brown sugar
- 1 teaspoon ground cinnamon
- 1/4 teaspoon ground nutmeg
- 2 tablespoons cider vinegar
- 2 tablespoons pure maple syrup
- 1 pinch salt

Instructions:
1. In a medium saucepan, combine apples, butter, brown sugar, cinnamon, and nutmeg. Cook over medium heat for about 5-7 minutes or until apples are just softened.
2. Add the vinegar and maple syrup and stir to combine. Simmer for 10 minutes more or until thick and syrupy.
3. Remove the pan from heat and stir in the salt. Pour the syrup into a jar or bottle and let cool before serving.

Nutrition information:
Calories: 110 kcal | Carbohydrates: 18 g | Protein: 0.7 g | Fat: 4.7 g | Saturated Fat: 3 g | Polyunsaturated Fat: 0 g | Monounsaturated Fat: 1.8 g | Sodium: 39 mg | Potassium: 25 mg | Fiber: 0.7 g | Sugar: 14 g | Vitamin A: 150 IU | Vitamin C: 0.9 mg | Calcium: 11 mg | Iron: 0.1 mg

101. Maple Bourbon Syrup

Sweeten up your pancakes and waffles with this homemade Maple Bourbon Syrup! It's simple to make and it has a hint of bourbon to give it extra flavor.
Serving: 4
Preparation time: 10 minutes
Ready time: 20 minutes

Ingredients:

1 cup pure maple syrup
2 tablespoons bourbon whiskey
1 teaspoon lemon juice
1/8 teaspoon ground cinnamon
1/8 teaspoon ground nutmeg

Instructions:
1. In a medium saucepan, combine maple syrup, bourbon, and lemon juice.
2. Cook over medium-low heat for 10 minutes, stirring frequently.
3. Stir in the cinnamon and nutmeg, and remove from heat.
4. Let the syrup cool slightly before serving.

Nutrition information: For 1/4 cup of maple bourbon syrup, the nutrition facts are: Calories: 138, Total Fat: 0g, Cholesterol: 0mg, Sodium: 4mg, Carbohydrates: 33g, Protein: 0g.

CONCLUSION

Syruplicious: 101 Homemade Recipes for Sweetening Your Life
has given readers the opportunity to explore the world of syrups
and learn how to make them from scratch at home. This cookbook
offers a variety of syrup recipes that range from savory to sweet to
delicious. From simple ingredients to complex flavor
combinations, each syrup has its own unique characteristics that
will bring an added sweetness to any dish. Whether it's adding a
touch of sweetness to dinner, enhancing desserts, or providing an
artistic flair to any food preparation, these syrups will not only add
a finishing flavor, but also a beautiful appearance.

The syrups in this cookbook serve as a unique way to experiment
with flavors, colors, and textures while creating dishes that are sure
to please. The extra amount of sugar or honey can add a depth of
flavor that can help turn a decent dish into a meal that is truly
memorable. It also provides a way to spice up a classic recipe or to
introduce a unique flavor to the dinner table. Using homemade
syrups, you can deliver the perfect balance of sweet and savory
flavor to any meal.

The recipes provided in this cookbook offer diverse options to
meet everyone's preference and dietary needs. It also includes ideas
for special occasions such as birthdays, anniversaries, or even
holidays. By preparing these syrups, each meal can be cradled in a
host of flavors that . satisfy the palate.

Syruplicious: 101 Homemade Recipes for Sweetening Your Life
offers an opportunity to anyone to satisfy their cravings and bring
a unique experience to the table. This cookbook encourages young
and old alike to explore the wonders of homemade syrups. Being
able to enjoy these syrups in cooking, in baking, or simply added
on top of a delightful dessert, is a charming way to enjoy mealtime.
With the recipes in this book, any meal becomes a special occasion
that will be remembered for generations to come. Syruplicious has
opened up many paths to make any occasion or meal extra special
and sweet.

Printed in Great Britain
by Amazon

44415922R00050